THE WORD AND THE BOMB

The Word and the Bomb

HANIF KUREISHI

faber and faber

First published in 2005
by Faber and Faber Limited
3 Queen Square, London WC1N 3AU

Typeset by Country Setting, Kingsdown, Kent CT14 8ES
Printed in England by Mackays of Chatham plc, Chatham, Kent

The right of Hanif Kureishi to be identified as author
of this work has been asserted in accordance with
Section 77 of the Copyright, Designs and Patents Act 1988

'The Rainbow Sign' was first published
with the screenplay of *My Beautiful Laundrette* in 1986.
'The Black Album' was first published in 1995.
'The Road Exactly' was first published
with the screenplay of *My Son the Fanatic* in 1998.
The story 'My Son the Fanatic' was first published
in a collection entitled *Love in a Blue Time* in 1997.
'Bradford' was first published in *Granta 20* (Winter 1986).
'Sex and Secularity' was first published as the introduction
to *Collected Screenplays One* in 2002.
'The Arduous Conversation Will Continue'
was first published in *The Guardian* in July 2005.
'The Carnival of Culture' was first published in July 2005.

A CIP record for this book
is available from the British Library

ISBN 0-571-23172-1

2 4 6 8 10 9 7 5 3 1

Contents

The Word and the Bomb

Most of the English writers I grew up reading were fascinated by the British Empire and the colonial idea, and they didn't hesitate to take it as their subject. E. M. Forster, Graham Greene, Evelyn Waugh, J. R. Ackerley, George Orwell and Anthony Burgess all tackled this area and its numerous implications in one way or another, for most of their writing lives.

As a young man, living in the London suburbs with an Indian father and English mother, I wanted to read works set in England, works that might help make sense of my own situation. Racism was real to me; the Empire was not. I liked Colin MacInnes and E. R. Braithwaite, whose *To Sir with Love* so moved me when I read it under the desk at school. But where were the British equivalents of the black American writers: James Baldwin, Richard Wright and Ralph Ellison? Who was noting the profound and permanent alterations to British life which had begun with the Empire and had now, as it were, come home?

Oddly, most modern British writers have been reluctant to similarly engage with such subjects at home. Questions of race, immigration, identity, Islam – the whole range of issues which so preoccupy us these days – have been absent from the work of my white contemporaries, even as a new generation of British writers has developed, following the lead of V. S. Naipaul and Salman Rushdie.

Most writers would say, quite rightly, that their subjects choose them; that they are interested in whatever they are interested in for reasons they cannot explain, and that writing is an experiment which takes you where it has to. The vocation of each writer is to describe the world as he or she sees it; anything more than that is advertising. Jo Shapcott puts it nicely in her poem 'The Mad Cow Talks Back': 'My brain's like the hive: constant little murmurs from its cells / saying this is the way, this is the way to go.'

In the post-war period, race – and now religion – have become subjects around which we discuss what is most important to us as individuals and as a society, and what scares us about others. Race is a reason to think about free speech and 'hate' speech; about integration, or what we have to be in order for society to work, and about the notion of the 'stranger'. We use the idea of race to think about education, and what we assume our children should know; about national identity: whether we need an identity at all, and what such an idea means; about sexuality, and the sexual attitudes and powers we ascribe to others, as well as our place in the world as a nation, and what our values are. We think, too, through the often mystifying topic of multiculturalism, about how mixed and mixed-up we are, so much so that we find it disconcerting for others to be multiple, and even worse, for us to be so, too. And because our politicians are so limited in what they can say and think, we need artists, intellectuals and academics to keep our cultural conversation going, to help us orient ourselves.

Yet a curious sort of literary apartheid has developed, with the latest 'post-colonial' generation exploring the racial and religious transformation of post-war Britain, while the rest leave the subject alone. When British television, cinema and theatre saw it as their duty to explore these issues – and the strangeness of the silence which often surrounded it – British writers of the generation following Graham Greene seemed scared of getting it wrong, of not understanding, even as they complained of having nothing 'important' to write about, envying American writers for having more compelling subjects.

Not that this apartheid was entirely innocent. Salman Rushdie, in a 1983 essay entitled 'Commonwealth Literature Does Not Exist', describes the attempt of the literature business to exclude certain writers, shoving them to the periphery under the patronising term 'Commonwealth writers'. The idea here is to keep writing in English pure, to change the terms of English literature 'into something far narrower, something topographical, nationalistic, possibly even racially segregationist'.

It isn't as though race is a new subject in Britain. Sukhdev Sandhu, in his comprehensive study *London Calling: How Black and Asian Writers Imagined a City*, quotes a correspondent for *The Times* in 1867: 'There is hardly such a thing as a pure Englishman in this island. In place of the rather vulgarised and very inaccurate phrase, "Anglo-Saxon", our national denomination, to be strictly correct, would be a composite of a dozen national titles.'

If, for E. M. Forster, the Empire was about power rather than mixing, its effect was permanently to alienate and separate people from one another. At the end of *A Passage to India*, the Englishman Fielding and his Muslim friend Aziz are out riding. Forster writes: 'Socially they had no meeting place. Would he today defy all his own people for the sake of a stray Indian? Aziz was a memento, a trophy, they were proud of each other, yet they must inevitably part.' Aziz himself cries, 'Clear out, all you Turtons and Burtons.' And, 'We shall drive every blasted Englishman into the sea!'

George Orwell takes a scalpel to this subject, telling us that political domination can only lead to humiliation, on both sides. In his essay 'Shooting an Elephant', the opening line of which is, 'In Moulmein, in Lower Burma, I was hated by large numbers of people – the only time in my life that I have been important enough for this to happen to me,' Orwell draws an uncompromising picture of how this humiliation works. Sent to kill a rogue elephant, a crowd of 'two thousand' begins to follows him, fascinated by how the Englishman will act. He feels himself to be 'an absurd puppet'; all that the natives want to do – 'the sneering yellow faces' – is laugh at him. But how could they respond otherwise? Later, writing about Kipling, he says, 'He does not see that the map is painted red chiefly in order that the coolie may be exploited.'

It is clear, in both Forster and Orwell, that the 'coloured' man is always inferior to the Englishman. He is not worth as much; he never will be. When it comes to character as well as colour, the white man is the gold standard. However, Orwell also saw that the Empire – and I guess he'd have applied this to immigration – was primarily economic. This was how countries enriched themselves. If the Empire wasn't supposed to be a moral crusade with the aim of making everyone alike, the only way to do it was to be ruthless – not half-hearted, as he was when called upon to dispose of the elephant. If the elephant is the Empire and Orwell the representative Englishman, he has to remove something that cannot easily be got rid of. And the elephant is with us still.

During my childhood and youth, differences in British society were always based around class and the conflicts they gave rise to. The Labour Party grew out of such clashes; its existence was based on them. But technology and consumerism became our gods. Now people are not even divided over politics, as there is only one party, and the opposition is fragmented, disorganised and without passion or direction. The real differences in Britain today are not political, or even based on class, but are arranged around race and religion, with their history of exploitation, humiliation and political helplessness.

Forster's Aziz got his wish: the British left the sub-continent. But in the vacuum following this hurried departure, there was political failure and dictatorship. Who, there, was seriously addressing the needs of the poor? For me, visiting Pakistan in the early 1980s, it was bewildering to hear older people wishing that Britain still ruled. Pakistan was becoming a theocracy and no one knew how to stop it. The Americans had been afraid of the Left, and hadn't noticed the significance of the mosques.

One of the most significant reasons for the rise of Islamic extremism in the Third World is the presence of financial and political corruption, along with the lack of free speech, and the failure to make a space for even the mildest political dissent. Pakistan, for instance, was a country constantly on the verge of collapse. My family in Karachi, along with most of the other middle-class families, hoarded their money in the West 'just in case', and educated their children in Britain and the US.

If the political class and the wealthy stole money, promoted their relatives – my Uncle Omar, a journalist in Pakistan, called it 'the son-in-law also rises' culture – and ensured that they had a route out, political dissent for those who did not have such privileges became organised around the mosque and the out-spoken clerics there. As with many revolutions, the route to free-dom from oppression also became the route to more oppression, to a familiar tyranny – that of the 'just' as opposed to that of the 'unjust'.

Young British Asians, the committed Muslims of *My Son the Fanatic* and *The Black Album*, were aware of this corruption at home and often felt guilty that they were in a better situation in the West. Corruption in their parents' land was also an injustice they wanted to repair.

The downfall of the Shah and the Iranian revolution of 1979, followed by a religious dictatorship, showed, at least, the effec-tiveness of Islam in fomenting political change. However, most people in the West became aware of the force and determination of radical Islam during the period of the fatwa against Rushdie, in 1989. Young Muslims told me that although they didn't succeed in either suppressing *The Satanic Verses* or eliminating its author, they were aware of how powerful their disapproval could be, and what energy they could create when organised. The Muslim writer Shabbir Akhtar admitted in *Be Careful with Muhammad* that, 'The Rushdie affair is, in the last analysis, admittedly about fanaticism on behalf of God.'

These young men were highly politicised and passionate. Believing they had unique access to virtue – and virtue was to be had only through submission to God – they were prepared to give up their lives for a cause. Forgetting how zealous we had once been about our own description of equality – socialism – we could only be shocked by their commitment and solidarity, and by their hatred of injustice, as well as their determination to bring about social change. We had not seen religious revolutionaries for a long time. Apart from liberation theology in South America – the church being used as an outlet for Left opposition – the only significant religion we saw for a long time was the soft New Age, as well as other right-wing cults, like the Moonies. Even Martin Luther King was considered by us to be a black leader rather than a religious one.

For us, religious commitment, particularly if it was political too, entailed not emancipation but a rejection of the Enlightenment and of modernity. How could we begin to deal with it? You respect people who are different, but how do you live with people who are so different that – among other things – they lock up their wives?

For young religious radicals, extreme Islam worked in many ways. It kept them out of trouble, for a start, and provided some pride. They weren't drinking, taking drugs, or getting into trouble like some of their white contemporaries. At the same time, they were able to be rebels. Being more fervent Muslims than their parents – and even condemning their parents – kept them within the Muslim fold, but enabled them to be transgressive at the same time. It's a difficult trick, to be simultaneously disobedient and conformist, but joining a cult or political organisation can fit both needs. The puritanical young can defy their fathers, but keep to the law of the ultimate Father. They are good, virtuous children, while rebelling.

Not that these young people are either representative or anything like the majority of Muslims in Britain. Earlier this year, making a short television documentary, I took a camera around the country and interviewed numerous Indian waiters. Having eaten in Indian restaurants all my life, I was fascinated by what these normally silent and unnoticed figures might say. To me, Indian restaurants with their sitar music, flocked wallpaper and pictures of the Taj Mahal on the wall, reproduced the colonial experience in this country for the ordinary person; the experience, of course, was 'Disneyfied', made bland and acceptable for the British, while retaining some of its charm.

Most of these waiters were keen on their work; feeding others was important for them. They had worked hard, and either they, or their families, had endured a traumatic transplantation to find a place in this country. They were Muslims; they prayed; they went to the mosque. But, as Shabbir Aktar says, 'For most Muslims, Islam is a "Friday religion".' The Islam they wanted was not incompatible with the West. The waiters wanted their

8

children – boys and girls alike – to be well-educated; they required a health service, housing and a democratic political structure. They were not segregated; they were important, well-known and respected in their town. They had multiple identities: being British, Bengali, and Welsh too. They were truly multicultural.

However, one of the waiters said to me recently, indicating his arm, his skin, his colour, 'Now they are blaming us all.' He wanted me to know he saw the present danger as a resurgence of racism, this time aimed specifically at Muslims. The idea might be to root out extremists, but a whole community may end up becoming stigmatised. One of the waiters mentioned his fear that rather than embodying the 'immigrant dream' of wealth, individuality and respect, they would become the permanent scapegoats of British society, as the blacks have become in the US. I have heard calls among the British for the re-installation of Englishness, as though there has been too much multiculturalism, rather than not enough. This wish for rigid, exclusive identities mirrors extreme Islam itself; it is an attempt to counter fundamentalism with more fundamentalism. This is a form of shame, when it is our excesses we should celebrate. We have been beset by bogeys before – Papists, communists, pornography – without losing our minds.

Not that mono-culturalism can work now: the world is too mixed. But there is the possibility of many new conflicts. After everything immigrants and their families have contributed to this country, the years of work and the racism faced, the war in Iraq, which Blair thought he could prosecute without cost or social division here, has brought more fragmentation. If Blair's 'third way' implies consensus and the end of antagonism, our literature will sharpen and map differences. 'Over-integration', the erasing of racial and religious differences, can become coercive or even fascistic. It can give rise to more racism, anger and resentment.

Edward Said wrote of the way Western writers constructed the East: the Orient as a convenient and simplistic fabrication, often as an obscene fantasy. Not that this is a fair picture of the work of writers like Forster or Orwell, who, from the inside, offered devastating critiques of their own class. Not that fantasies don't go both ways. Among Muslims, there has been a reverse Orientalism, or 'Occidentalism', at work. Many of the fundamentalists I met, indeed many Muslims, were keen to see the West as corrupt and over-sexualised; there was 'too much freedom'. The West could seem chaotic, over-individualistic; the family was less important, or constantly mutating. These Muslims refused to look at Western culture and science, or the institutions which can only flourish in a relatively free atmosphere, preferring to see the inevitable underside: addiction, divorce, social breakdown.

In the light of such deliberate mutual incomprehension, we might ask ourselves what the use of writing is. However, you might as well ask what the use of speaking or telling stories is. Edward Said identified useful writing as 'speaking the truth to power'. The attacks on Rushdie show us, at least, that the Word is dangerous, and that independent and critical thought is more important than ever. In an age of propaganda, political simplicities and violence, our stories are crucial. Apart from the fact that the political has to be constantly interrogated, it is in such stories – which are conversations with ourselves – that we can speak of, include and generate more complex and difficult selves. It is when the talking and writing stops, when the attempt is to suppress human inconsistency by virtue, that evil takes place in the silence. The antidote to puritanism isn't licentiousness, but recognition of what goes on inside human beings. Fundamentalism is dictatorship of the mind, but a live culture is an exploration, and represents our endless curiosity about our own strangeness and impossible sexuality: wisdom is more important than doctrine; doubt more important than certainty. Fundamentalism implies the failure of our most significant attribute, our imagination. In the fundamentalist scheme there is only one imaginer – God. The rest of us are his servants.

The freedom to speak is not only our privilege, but is essential to the oppressed, unheard and marginalised of the Third World, as they struggle to keep their humanity alive in conditions far worse than here. To retreat into a citadel of 'Englishness', to refuse to link up or identify with them, is to deliver them over to superstition and poverty of the imagination.

The Rushdie case remains instructive. In the end it is Islam itself which suffers from the repudiation of more sensual and dissident ideas of itself. Shabbir Akhtar – and his like – cannot understand that by leaving out, or attempting to suppress, so much of themselves, by parting company from an essential component of their own heritage, they are losing access to a source of enjoyment, energy and understanding. Radical Islam, then, far from looking like a new revolutionary movement, has come to rather resemble other totalitarian systems like Catholicism and communism, neither of which – under the rule of dull old men – could see the value of obscenity.

Immorality and blasphemy require protection. The roll-call of the censored is an account of our civilisation. If Islam is incapable of making any significant contribution to culture and knowledge, it is because extreme puritanism and censoriousness can only lead to a paranoia which will cause it to become more violent and unable to speak for those it is intended to serve. That which we seek to exclude returns to haunt us.

The pieces which follow – from 'The Rainbow Sign' in 1986 to articles written for the *Guardian* in the aftermath of the London bombings in July 2005 – reflect the evolution of my thinking about the conflict between Islam and Western liberalism over the past two decades.

The Rainbow Sign

(1986)

'God gave Noah the rainbow sign,
No more water, the fire next time!'

ONE: ENGLAND

I was born in London of an English mother and Pakistani father. My father, who lives in London, came to England from Bombay in 1947 to be educated by the old colonial power. He married here and never went back to India. The rest of his large family, his brothers, their wives, his sisters, moved from Bombay to Karachi, in Pakistan, after partition.

Frequently during my childhood, I met my Pakistani uncles when they came to London on business. They were important, confident people who took me to hotels, restaurants and test matches, often in taxis. But I had no idea of what the sub-continent was like or how my numerous uncles, aunts and cousins lived there. When I was nine or ten a teacher purposefully placed some pictures of Indian peasants in mud huts in front of me and said to the class: 'Hanif comes from India.' I wondered: did my uncles ride on camels? Surely not in their suits? Did my cousins, so like me in other ways, squat down in the sand like little Mowglis, half-naked and eating with their fingers?

In the mid-1960s, Pakistanis were a risible subject in England, derided on television and exploited by politicians. They had the worst jobs, they were uncomfortable in England, some of them had difficulties with the language. They were despised and out of place.

From the start I tried to deny my Pakistani self. I was ashamed. It was a curse and I wanted to be rid of it. I wanted to be like everyone else. I read with understanding a story in a newspaper about a black boy who, when he noticed that burnt skin turned white, jumped into a bath of boiling water.

At school, one teacher always spoke to me in a 'Peter Sellers' Indian accent. Another refused to call me by my name, calling me Pakistani Pete instead. So I refused to call the teacher by *his* name and used his nickname instead. This led to trouble; arguments, detentions, escapes from school over hedges and, eventually, suspension. This played into my hands; this couldn't have been better.

With a friend I roamed the streets and fields all day; I sat beside streams; I stole yellow lurex trousers from a shop and smuggled them out of the house under my school trousers; I hid in woods reading hard books; and I saw the film *Zulu* several times.

This friend, who became Johnny in my film, *My Beautiful Laundrette*, came one day to the house. It was a shock.

He was dressed in jeans so tough they almost stood up by themselves. These were suspended above his boots by Union Jack braces of 'hangman's strength', revealing a stretch of milk-bottle white leg. He seemed to have sprung up several inches because of his Doctor Martens boots, which had steel caps and soles as thick as cheese sandwiches. His Ben Sherman shirt with a pleat down the back was essential. And his hair, which was only a quarter of an inch long all over, stuck out of his head like little nails. This unmoving creation he concentratedly touched up every hour with a sharpened steel comb that also served as a dagger.

He soon got the name Bog Brush, though this was not a moniker you would use to his face. Where before he was an angel-boy with a blond quiff flattened down by his mother's loving spit, a clean handkerchief always in his pocket, as well as being a keen cornet player for the Air Cadets, he'd now gained a brand new truculent demeanour.

My mother was so terrified by this storm trooper dancing on her doorstep to the 'Skinhead Moonstomp', which he moaned to himself continuously, that she had to lie down.

I decided to go out roaming with B.B. before my father got home from work. But it wasn't the same as before. We couldn't have our talks without being interrupted. Bog Brush had become Someone. To his intense pleasure, similarly dressed strangers greeted Bog Brush in the street as if they were in a war-torn foreign country and in the same army battalion. We were suddenly banned from cinemas. The Wimpy Bar in which we sat for hours with milkshakes wouldn't let us in. As a matter of pride we now had to go round the back and lob a brick at the rear window of the place.

Other strangers would spot us from the other side of the street. B.B. would yell 'Leg it!' as the enemy dashed through traffic and leapt over the bonnets of cars to get at us, screaming obscenities and chasing us up alleys, across allotments, around reservoirs, and on and on.

And then, in the evening, B.B. took me to meet with the other lads. We climbed the park railings and strolled across to the football pitch, by the goalposts. This is where the lads congregated to hunt down Pakistanis and beat them. Most of them I was at school with. The others I'd grown up with. I knew their parents. They knew my father.

I withdrew, from the park, from the lads, to a safer place, within myself. I moved into what I call my 'temporary' period. I was only waiting now to get away, to leave the London suburbs, to make another kind of life, somewhere else, with better people.

In this isolation, in my bedroom where I listened to the Pink Floyd, the Beatles and the John Peel show, I started to write down the speeches of politicians, the words which helped create the neo-Nazi attitudes I saw around me. This I called 'keeping the accounts'.

In 1965, Enoch Powell said: 'We should not lose sight of the desirability of achieving a steady flow of voluntary repatriation for the elements which are proving unsuccessful or unassimilable.'

In 1967, Duncan Sandys said: 'The breeding of millions of half-caste children would merely produce a generation of misfits and create national tensions.'

I wasn't a misfit; I could join the elements of myself together. It was the others, they wanted misfits; they wanted you to embody within yourself their ambivalence.

Also in 1967, Enoch Powell – who once said he would love to have been Viceroy of India – quoted a constituent of his as saying that because of the Pakistanis 'this country will not be worth living in for our children'.

And Powell said, more famously: 'As I look ahead I am filled with foreboding. Like the Roman, "I seem to see the River Tiber foaming with much blood".'

As Powell's speeches appeared in the papers, graffiti in support of him appeared in the London streets. Racists gained confidence. People insulted me in the street. Someone in a café refused to eat at the same table with me. The parents of a girl I was in love with told her she'd get a bad reputation by going out with darkies.

Powell allowed himself to become a figurehead for racists. He helped create racism in Britain and was directly responsible not only for the atmosphere of fear and hatred, but through his influence, for individual acts of violence against Pakistanis.

Television comics used Pakistanis as the butt of their humour. Their jokes were highly political: they contributed to a way of seeing the world. The enjoyed reduction of racial hatred to a joke did two things: it expressed a collective view (which was sanctioned by its being on the BBC), and it was a celebration of contempt in millions of living rooms in England. I was afraid to watch TV because of it; it was too embarrassing, too degrading.

Parents of my friends, both lower-middle-class and working-class, often told me they were Powell supporters. Sometimes I heard them talking, heatedly, violently, about race, about 'the Pakis'. I was desperately embarrassed and afraid of being identified with these loathed aliens. I found it almost impossible to answer questions about where I came from. The word 'Pakistani' had been made into an insult. It was a word I didn't want used about myself. I couldn't tolerate being myself.

The British complained incessantly that the Pakistanis wouldn't assimilate. This meant they wanted the Pakistanis to be exactly like them. But of course even then they would have rejected them.

The British were doing the assimilating: they assimilated Pakistanis to their world view. They saw them as dirty, ignorant and less than human – worthy of abuse and violence.

At this time I found it difficult to get along with anyone. I was frightened and hostile. I suspected that my white friends were capable of racist insults. And many of them did taunt me, innocently. I reckoned that at least once every day since I was five years old I had been racially abused. I became incapable of distinguishing between remarks that were genuinely intended to hurt and those intended as 'humour'.

I became cold and distant. I began to feel I was very violent. But I didn't know how to be violent. If I had known, if that had come naturally to me, or if there'd been others I could follow, I would have made my constant fantasies of revenge into realities, I would have got into trouble, willingly hurt people, or set fire to things.

But I mooched around libraries. There, in an old copy of *Life* magazine, I found pictures of the Black Panthers. It was Eldridge Cleaver, Huey Newton, Bobby Seale and their confederates in black vests and slacks, with Jimi Hendrix haircuts. Some of them were holding guns, the Army .45 and the 12-gauge Magnum shotgun with 18-inch barrel that Huey specified for street fighting.

I tore down my pictures of the Rolling Stones and Cream and replaced them with the Panthers. I found it all exhilarating. These people were proud and they were fighting. To my knowledge, no one in England was fighting.

There was another, more important picture.

On the cover of the Penguin edition of *The Fire Next Time* was James Baldwin holding a child, his nephew. Baldwin, having suffered, having been there, was all anger and understanding. He was intelligence and love combined. As I planned my escape I read Baldwin all the time, I read Richard Wright and I admired Muhammad Ali.

A great moment occurred when I was in a sweet shop. I saw through to a TV in the backroom on which was showing the 1968 Olympic Games in Mexico. Thommie Smith and John Carlos were raising their fists on the victory rostrum, giving the Black Power salute as the 'Star Spangled Banner' played. The white shopkeeper was outraged. He said to me: they shouldn't mix politics and sport.

During this time there was always Muhammad Ali, the former Cassius Clay. a great sportsman become black spokesman. Now a Muslim, millions of fellow Muslims all over the world prayed for his victory when he fought.

And there was the Nation of Islam movement to which Ali belonged, led by the man who called himself the Messenger of Islam and wore a gold-embroidered fez, Elijah Muhammad.

Elijah was saying in the mid-1960s that the rule of the white devils would end in fifteen years. He preached separatism, separate development for black and white. He ran his organisation by charisma and threat, claiming that anyone who challenged him would be chastened by Allah. Apparently Allah also turned the minds of defectors into a turmoil.

Elijah's disciple Malcolm X, admirer of Gandhi and self-confirmed anti-Semite, accepted in prison that 'the key to a Muslim is submission, the attunement of one towards Allah'. That this glorious resistance to the white man, the dismissal of Christian meekness, was followed by submission to Allah and worse, to Elijah Muhammad, was difficult to take.

I saw racism as unreason and prejudice, ignorance and a failure of sense; it was Fanon's 'incomprehension'. That the men I wanted to admire had liberated themselves only to take to unreason, to the abdication of intelligence, was shocking to me. And the separatism, the total loathing of the white man as innately corrupt, the 'All whites are devils' view, was equally unacceptable. I had to live in England, in the suburbs of London, with whites. My mother was white. I wasn't ready for separate development. I'd had too much of that already.

Luckily James Baldwin wasn't too keen either. In *The Fire Next Time* he describes a visit to Elijah Muhammad. He tells of how close he feels to Elijah and how he wishes to be able to love him. But when he tells Elijah that he has many white friends, he receives Elijah's pity. For Elijah the whites' time is up. It's no good Baldwin telling him he has white friends with whom he'd entrust his life.

As the evening goes on, Baldwin tires of the sycophancy around

Elijah. He and Elijah would always be strangers and 'possibly enemies'. Baldwin deplores the black Muslims' turning to Africa and to Islam, this turning away from the reality of America and 'inventing' the past. Baldwin also mentions Malcolm X and the chief of the American Nazi party saying that racially speaking they were in complete agreement: they both wanted separate development. Baldwin adds that the debasement of one race and the glorification of another in this way inevitably leads to murder.

After this the Muslims weren't too keen on Baldwin, to say the least. Eldridge Cleaver, who once raped white women 'on principle', had a picture of Elijah Muhammad, the great strength-giver, on his prison wall. Later he became a devoted supporter of Malcolm X.

Cleaver says of Baldwin: 'There is in James Baldwin's work the most gruelling, agonising, total hatred of the blacks, particularly of himself, and the most shameful, fanatical, fawning, sycophantic love of the whites that one can find in the writing of any black American writer of note in our time.'

How strange it was to me, this worthless abuse of a writer who could enter the minds and skins of both black and white, and the good just anger turning to passionate Islam as a source of pride instead of to a digested political commitment to a different kind of whole society. And this easy, thrilling talk of 'white devils' instead of close analysis of the institutions that kept blacks low.

I saw the taking up of Islam as an aberration, a desperate fantasy of worldwide black brotherhood; it was a symptom of extreme alienation. It was also an inability to seek a wider political view or cooperation with other oppressed groups – or with the working class as a whole – since alliance with white groups was necessarily out of the question.

I had no idea what an Islamic society would be like, what the application of the authoritarian theology Elijah preached would mean in practice. I forgot about it, fled the suburbs, went to university, got started as a writer and worked as an usher at the

Royal Court Theatre. It was over ten years before I went to an Islamic country.

TWO: PAKISTAN

The man had heard that I was interested in talking about his country, Pakistan, and that this was my first visit. He kindly kept trying to take me aside to talk. But I was already being talked to.

I was at another Karachi party, in a huge house, with a glass of whisky in one hand, and a paper plate in the other. Casually I'd mentioned to a woman friend of the family that I wasn't against marriage. Now this friend was earnestly recommending to me a young woman who wanted to move to Britain, with a husband. To my discomfort this go-between was trying to fix a time for the three of us to meet and negotiate.

I went to three parties a week in Karachi. This time, when I could get away from this woman, I was with landowners, diplomats, businessmen and politicians: powerful people. This pleased me. They were people I wouldn't have been able to get to in England and I wanted to write about them.

They were drinking heavily. Every liberal in England knows you can be lashed for drinking in Pakistan. But as far as I could tell, none of this English-speaking international bourgeoisie would be lashed for anything. They all had their favourite trusted bootleggers who negotiated the potholes of Karachi at high speed on disintegrating motorcycles, with the hooch stashed on the back. Bad bootleggers passed a hot needle through the neck of your bottle and drew your whisky out. Stories were told of guests politely sipping ginger beer with their ice and soda, glancing at other guests to see if they were drunk and wondering if their own alcohol tolerance had miraculously increased.

I once walked into a host's bathroom to see the bath full of floating whisky bottles being soaked to remove the labels, a servant sitting on a stool serenely poking at them with a stick.

So it was all as tricky and expensive as buying cocaine in

London, with the advantage that as the hooch market was so competitive, the 'leggers delivered video tapes at the same time, dashing into the room towards the TV with hot copies of *The Jewel in the Crown, The Far Pavilions* and an especially popular programme called *Mind Your Language,* which represented Indians and Pakistanis as ludicrous caricatures.

Everyone, except the mass of the population, had videos. And I could see why, since Pakistan TV was so peculiar. On my first day I turned it on and a cricket match was taking place. I settled in my chair. But the English players, who were on tour in Pakistan, were leaving the pitch. In fact, Bob Willis and Ian Botham were running towards the dressing rooms surrounded by armed police and this wasn't because Botham had made derogatory remarks about Pakistan. (He said it was a country to which he'd like to send his mother-in-law.) In the background a section of the crowd was being tear-gassed. Then the screen went blank.

Stranger still, and more significant, was the fact that the news was now being read in Arabic, a language few people in Pakistan understood. Someone explained to me that this was because the Koran was in Arabic, but everyone else said it was because General Zia wanted to kiss the arses of the Arabs.

The man at the party, who was drunk, wanted to tell me something and kept pulling at me. The man was worried. But wasn't I worried too? I was trapped with this woman and the marriage proposal.

I was having a little identity crisis. I'd been greeted so warmly in Pakistan, I felt so excited by what I saw, and so at home with all my uncles, I wondered if I were not better off here than there. And when I said, with a little unnoticed irony, that I was an Englishman, people laughed. They fell about. Why would anyone with a brown face, Muslim name and large well-known family in Pakistan want to lay claim to that cold little decrepit island off Europe where you always had to spell your name? Strangely, anti-British remarks made me feel patriotic, though I only felt patriotic when I was away from England.

But I couldn't allow myself to feel too Pakistani. I didn't want to give in to that falsity, that sentimentality. As someone said to me at a party, provoked by the fact I was wearing jeans: we are Pakistanis, but you, you will always be a Paki – emphasising the slang derogatory name the English used against Pakistanis, and therefore the fact that I couldn't rightfully lay claim to either place.

In England I was a playwright. In Karachi this meant little. There were no theatres; the arts were discouraged by the state – music and dancing are un-Islamic – and ignored by practically everyone else. So despite everything I felt pretty out of place.

The automatic status I gained through my family obtained for me such acceptance, respect and luxury that for the first time I could understand the privileged and their penchant for marshalling ridiculous arguments to justify their delicious and untenable position as an elite. But as I wasn't a doctor, or businessman or military person, people suspected that this writing business I talked about was a complicated excuse for idleness, uselessness and general bumming around. In fact, as I proclaimed an interest in the entertainment business, and talked much and loudly about how integral the arts were to a society, moves were being made to set me up in the amusement arcade business, in Shepherd's Bush.

Finally the man got me on my own. His name was Rahman. He was a friend of my intellectual uncle. I had many uncles, but Rahman preferred the intellectual one who understood Rahman's particular sorrow and like him considered himself to be a marginal man.

In his fifties, a former Air Force officer, Rahman was liberal, well-travelled and married to an Englishwoman who now had a Pakistani accent.

He said to me: 'I tell you, this country is being sodomised by religion. It is even beginning to interfere with the making of money. And now we are embarked on this dynamic regression, you must know, it is obvious, Pakistan has become a leading country to go away from. Our patriots are abroad. We despise and envy them. For the rest of us, our class, your family, we are in Hobbes's state of nature: insecure, frightened. We cling together out of necessity.' He became optimistic. 'We could be like Japan, a tragic oriental country that is now progressive, industrialised.' He laughed and then said, ambiguously: 'But only God keeps this country together. You must say this around the world: we are taking a great leap backwards.'

The bitterest blow for Rahman was the dancing. He liked to waltz and foxtrot. But now the expression of physical joy, of sensuality and rhythm, was banned. On TV you could see where it had been censored. When couples in Western programmes got up to dance, there'd be a jerk in the film and they'd be sitting down again. For Rahman it was inexplicable, an unnecessary cruelty that was almost more arbitrary than anything else.

Thus the despair of Rahman and my uncles' 'high and dry' generation. Mostly educated in Britain, like Jinnah, the founder of Pakistan – who was a smoking, drinking, non-Urdu-speaking lawyer and claimed that Pakistan would never be a theocracy ('that Britisher' he was sometimes called) – their intellectual mentors were Tawney, Shaw, Russell, Laski. For them the new Islamisation was the negation of their lives.

It was a lament I heard often. This was the story they told. Karachi was a goodish place in the 1960s and 1970s. Until about 1977 it was lively and vigorous. You could drink and dance in the Raj-style clubs (providing you were admitted) and the atmosphere was liberal – as long as you didn't meddle in politics, in which case you'd probably be imprisoned. Politically there was Bhutto: urbane, Oxford-educated, considering himself to be a poet and revolutionary, a veritable Chairman Mao of the subcontinent. He said he would fight obscurantism and illiteracy, ensure the equality of men and women, and increase access to education and medical care. The desert would bloom.

Later, in an attempt to save himself, appease the mullahs and rouse the dissatisfied masses behind him, he introduced various Koranic injunctions into the constitution and banned alcohol, gambling, horseracing. The Islamisation had begun, and was fervently continued after his execution.

Islamisation built no hospitals, no schools, no houses; it cleaned no water and installed no electricity. But it was direction, identity. The country was to be in the hands of the divine, or rather, in the hands of those who elected themselves to interpret the single divine purpose. Under the tyranny of the priesthood, with the cooperation of the army, Pakistan would embody Islam in itself.

There would now be no distinction between ethical and religious obligation; there would now be no areas in which it was possible to be wrong. The only possible incertitude was of interpretation. The theory would be the written eternal and universal principles which Allah created and made obligatory for men; the model would be the first three generations of Muslims; and the practice would be Pakistan.

As a Professor of Law at the Islamic University wrote: 'Pakistan accepts Islam as the basis of economic and political life. We do not have a single reason to make any separation between Islam and Pakistan society. Pakistanis now adhere rigorously to Islam and cling steadfastly to their religious heritage. They never speak of these things with disrespect. With an acceleration in the process of Islamisation, governmental capabilities increase and national identity and loyalty become stronger. Because Islamic civilisation has brought Pakistanis very close to certainty, this society is ideally imbued with a moral mission.'

This moral mission and the over-emphasis on dogma and punishment resulted in the kind of strengthening of the repressive, militaristic and nationalistically aggressive state seen all over the world in the authoritarian 1980s. With the added bonus that, in Pakistan, God was always on the side of the government.

But despite all the strident nationalism, as Rahman said, the patriots were abroad; people were going away: to the West, to Saudi Arabia, anywhere. Young people continually asked me about the possibility of getting into Britain, and some thought of taking some smack with them to bankroll their establishment. They had what was called the Gulf Syndrome, a condition I recognised from my time living in the suburbs. It was a dangerous psychological cocktail consisting of ambition, suppressed excitement, bitterness and sexual longing.

Then a disturbing incident occurred which seemed to encapsulate the going-away fever. An eighteen-year-old girl from a village called Chakwal dreamed that the villagers walked across the Arabian Sea to Karbala where they found money and work. Following this dream the village set off one night for the beach which happened to be near my uncle's house, in fashionable Clifton. Here lived politicians and diplomats in LA-style white bungalows with sprinklers on the lawn, a Mercedes in the drive and dogs and watchmen at the gates.

Here Benazir Bhutto was under house arrest. Her dead father's mansion was patrolled by the army who boredly nursed machine guns and sat in tents beneath the high walls.

On the beach, the site of barbecues and late-night parties, the men of the Chakwal village packed the women and children into trunks and pushed them into the Arabian Sea. Then they followed them into the water, in the direction of Karbala. All but twenty of the potential *émigrés* were drowned. The survivors were arrested and charged with illegal emigration.

It was the talk of Karachi. It caused much amusement but people like Rahman despaired of a society that could be so confused, so advanced in some respects, so very naive in others.

And all the (more orthodox) going away disturbed and confused the family set-up. When the men who'd been away came back, they were different, they were dissatisfied, they had seen more, they wanted more. Their neighbours were envious and resentful. Once more the society was being changed by outside forces, not by its own volition.

About twelve people lived permanently in my uncle's house, plus servants who slept in sheds at the back, just behind the chickens and dogs. Relatives sometimes came to stay for months. New bits had to be built on to the house. All day there were visitors; in the evenings crowds of people came over; they were welcome, and they ate and watched videos and talked for hours. People weren't so protective of their privacy as they were in London.

This made me think about the close-bonding within the families and about the intimacy and interference of an extended family and a more public way of life. Was the extended family worse than the little nuclear family because there were more people to dislike? Or better because relationships were less intense?

Strangely, bourgeois-bohemian life in London, in Notting Hill and Islington and Fulham, was far more formal. It was frozen dinner parties and the division of social life into the meeting of couples with other couples, to discuss the lives of other coupling couples. Months would pass, then this would happen again.

In Pakistan, there was the continuity of the various families' knowledge of each other. People were easy to place; your grandparents and theirs were friends. When I went to the bank and showed the teller my passport, it turned out he knew several of my uncles, so I didn't receive the usual perfunctory treatment. This was how things worked.

I compared the collective hierarchy of the family and the permanence of my family's circle, with my feckless, rather rootless life in London, in what was called 'the inner city'. There I lived alone, and lacked any long connection with anything. I'd hardly known anyone for more than eight years, and certainly not their parents. People came and went. There was much false intimacy and forced friendship. People didn't take responsibility for each other.

Many of my friends lived alone in London, especially the women. They wanted to be independent and to enter into relationships – as many as they liked, with whom they liked – out of choice. They didn't merely want to reproduce the old patterns of living. The future was to be determined by choice and reason, not by custom. The notions of duty and obligation barely had positive meaning for my friends; they were loaded, Victorian words, redolent of constraint and grandfather clocks, the antithesis of generosity in love, the new hugging, and the transcendence of the family. The ideal of the new relationship was no longer the S and M of the old marriage – it was F and C, freedom plus commitment.

In the large, old families where there was nothing but the old patterns, disturbed only occasionally by the new ways, this would have seemed a contrivance, a sort of immaturity, a failure to understand and accept the determinacies that life necessarily involved.

So there was much pressure to conform, especially on the women.

'Let these women be warned,' said a mullah to the dissenting women of Rawalpindi. 'We will tear them to pieces. We will give them such terrible punishments that no one in future will dare to raise a voice against Islam.'

I remember a woman saying to me at dinner one night: 'We know at least one thing. God will never dare to show his face in this country – the women will tear him apart!'

The family scrutiny and criticism was difficult to take, as was all the bitching and gossip. But there was warmth and continuity for a large number of people; there was security and much love. Also there was a sense of duty and community – of people's lives genuinely being lived together, whether they liked each other or not – that you didn't get in London. There, those who'd eschewed the family hadn't succeeded in creating some other form of supportive common life. In Pakistan there was that supportive common life, but at the expense of movement and change.

In the 1960s of Enoch Powell and graffiti, the Black Muslims and Malcolm X gave needed strength to the descendants of slaves by 'taking the wraps off the white man'; Eldridge Cleaver was yet to be converted to Christianity and Huey P. Newton was toting his Army .45. A boy in a bedroom in a suburb, who had the King's Road constantly on his mind and who changed the pictures on his wall from week to week, was unhappy, and separated from the 1960s as by a thick glass wall against which he could only press his face. But bits of the 1960s were still around in Pakistan: the liberation rhetoric, for example, the music, the clothes, the drugs, not as the way of life they were originally intended to be, but as appendages to another, stronger tradition.

As my friends and I went into the Bara Market near Peshawar, close to the border of Afghanistan, in a rattling motorised rickshaw, I became apprehensive. There were large signs by the road telling foreigners that the police couldn't take responsibility for them: beyond this point the police would not go. Apparently the Pathans there, who were mostly refugees from Afghanistan, liked to kidnap foreigners and extort ransoms. My friends, who were keen to buy opium, which they'd give to the rickshaw driver to carry, told me everything was all right, because I wasn't a foreigner. I kept forgetting that.

The men were tough, martial, insular and proud. They lived in mud houses and tin shacks built like forts for shooting from. They were inevitably armed, with machine guns slung over their shoulders. In the street you wouldn't believe women existed here, except you knew they took care of the legions of young men in the area who'd fled from Afghanistan to avoid being conscripted by the Russians and sent to Moscow for re-education.

Ankle-deep in mud, I went round the market. Pistols, knives, Russian-made rifles, hand grenades and large lumps of dope and opium were laid out on stalls like tomatoes and oranges. Everyone was selling heroin.

The Americans, who had much money invested in Pakistan, in this compliant right-wing buffer-zone between Afghanistan and India, were furious that their children were being destroyed by a flourishing illegal industry in a country they financed. But the Americans sent to Pakistan could do little about it. Involvement in the heroin trade went right through Pakistan society: the police, the judiciary, the army, the landlords, the customs officials were all involved. After all, there was nothing in the Koran about heroin, nothing specific. I was even told that its export made ideological sense. Heroin was anti-Western; addiction in Western children was a deserved symptom of the moral vertigo of godless societies. It was a kind of colonial revenge. Reverse imperialism, the Karachi wits called it, inviting nemesis. The reverse imperialism was itself being reversed.

In a flat high above Karachi, an eighteen-year-old kid strung out on heroin danced cheerfully around the room in front of me and pointed to an erection in the front of his trousers, which he referred to as his Imran Khan, the name of the handsome Pakistan cricket captain. More and more of the so-called multi-national kids were taking heroin now. My friends who owned the flat, journalists on a weekly paper, were embarrassed.

But they always had dope to offer their friends. These laid-back people were mostly professionals: lawyers, an inspector in the police who smoked what he confiscated, a newspaper magnate, and various other journalists. Heaven it was to smoke at midnight on the beach, as local fishermen, squatting respect-fully behind you, fixed fat joints; and the 'erotic politicians' themselves, the Doors, played from a portable stereo while the Arabian Sea rolled on to the beach. Oddly, since heroin and dope were both indigenous to the country, it took the West to make them popular in the East.

In so far as colonisers and colonised engage in a relationship with the latter aspiring to be like the former, you wouldn't catch anyone of my uncle's generation with a joint in their mouth. It was *infra dig* – for the peasants. Shadowing the British, they drank whisky and read *The Times*; they praised others by calling them 'gentlemen'; and their eyes filled with tears at old Vera Lynn records.

But the kids discussed yoga exercises. You'd catch them standing on their heads. They even meditated. Though one boy who worked at the airport said it was too much of a Hindu thing for Muslims to be doing; if his parents caught him chanting a mantra he'd get a backhander across the face. Mostly the kids listened to the Stones, Van Morrison and Bowie as they flew over ruined roads to the beach in bright red and yellow Japanese cars with quadrophonic speakers, past camels and acres of wasteland.

Here, all along the railway track, the poor and diseased and hungry lived in shacks and huts; the filthy poor gathered around rusty standpipes to fetch water; or ingeniously they resurrected wrecked cars, usually Morris Minors; and here they slept in huge sewer pipes among buffalo, chickens and wild dogs. Here I met a policeman who I thought was on duty. But the policeman lived here, and hanging on the wall of his falling-down shed was his spare white police uniform, which he'd had to buy himself.

If not to the beach, the kids went to the Happy Hamburger to hang out. Or to each other's houses to watch Clint Eastwood tapes and giggle about sex, of which they were so ignorant and deprived. I watched a group of agitated young men in their mid-twenties gather around a 1950s medical book to look at the female genitalia. For these boys, who watched Western films and mouthed the lyrics of pop songs celebrating desire ('Come on, baby, light my fire'), life before marriage could only be like spending years and years in a single-sex public school; for them women were mysterious, unknown, desirable and yet threatening creatures of almost another species, whom you had to respect, marry and impregnate but couldn't be friends with. And in this country where the sexes were usually strictly segregated, the sexual tension could be palpable. The men who could afford to flew to Bangkok for relief. The others squirmed and resented women. The kind of sexual openness that was one of the few real achievements of the 1960s, the discussion of contraception, abortion, female sexuality and prostitution which some women were trying to advance, received incredible hostility. But women felt it was only a matter of time before progress was made; it was much harder to return to ignorance than the mullahs thought.

A stout intense lawyer in his early thirties of immense extrovert charm – with him it was definitely the 1980s, not the 1960s. His father was a judge. He himself was intelligent, articulate and fiercely representative of the other 'new spirit' of Pakistan. He didn't drink, smoke or fuck. Out of choice. He prayed five times a day. He worked all the time. He was determined to be a good Muslim, since that was the whole point of the country existing at all. He wasn't indulgent, except religiously, and he lived in accordance with what he believed. I took to him immediately.

We had dinner in an expensive restaurant. It could have been in London or New York. The food was excellent, I said. The lawyer disagreed, with his mouth full, shaking his great head. It was definitely no good, it was definitely meretricious rubbish. But for ideological reasons only, I concluded, since he ate with relish. He was only in the restaurant because of me, he said.

There was better food in the villages; the new food in Pakistan was, frankly. a tribute to chemistry rather than cuisine. Only the masses had virtue, they knew how to live, how to eat. He told me that those desiccated others, the marginal men I associated with and liked so much, were a plague class with no values. Perhaps, he suggested, eating massively, this was why I liked them, being English. Their education, their intellectual snobbery, made them un-Islamic. They didn't understand the masses and they spoke in English to cut themselves off from the people. Didn't the best jobs go to those with a foreign education? He was tired of those Westernised elders denigrating their country and its religious nature. They'd been contaminated by the West, they didn't know their own country, and the sooner they got out and were beaten up by racists abroad the better.

The lawyer and I went out into the street. It was busy, the streets full of strolling people. There were dancing camels and a Pakistan trade exhibition. The lawyer strode through it all, yelling. The exhibition was full of Pakistan-made imitations of Western goods: bathrooms in chocolate and strawberry, TVs with stereos attached; fans, air-conditioners, heaters; and an arcade full of space-invaders. The lawyer got agitated.

These were Western things, of no use to the masses. The masses didn't have water, what would they do with strawberry bathrooms? The masses wanted Islam, not space-invaders or . . . or elections. Are elections a Western thing? I asked. Don't they have them in India too? No, they're a Western thing, the lawyer said. How could they be required under Islam? There need only be one party – the party of the righteous.

This energetic lawyer would have pleased and then disappointed Third World intellectuals and revolutionaries from an earlier era, people like Fanon and Guevara. This talk of liberation – at last the acknowledgement of the virtue of the toiling masses, the struggle against neo-colonialism, its bourgeois stooges and American interference – the entire recognisable rhetoric of freedom and struggle, ends in the lawyer's mind with the country on its knees, at prayer. Having started to look for itself it finds itself . . . in the eighth century.

Islam and the masses. My numerous meetings with scholars, revisionists, liberals who wanted the Koran 'creatively' interpreted to make it compatible with modern science. The many medieval monologues of mullahs I'd listened to. So much talk, theory and Byzantine analysis.

I strode into a room in my uncle's house. Half-hidden by a curtain, on a verandah, was an aged woman servant wearing my cousin's old clothes, praying. I stopped and watched her. In the morning, as I lay in bed, she swept the floor of my room with some twigs bound together. She was at least sixty. Now, on the shabby prayer mat, she was tiny and around her the universe was endless, immense, but God was above her. I felt she was acknowledging that which was larger than her, humbling herself before the infinite, knowing and feeling her own insignificance. It was a truthful moment, not empty ritual. I wished I could do it.

I went with the lawyer to the Mosque in Lahore, the largest in the world. I took off my shoes, padded across the immense courtyard with the other men – women were not allowed – and got on my knees. I banged my forehead on the marble floor. Beside me a man in a similar posture gave a world-consuming yawn. I waited but could not lose myself in prayer. I could only travesty the woman's prayer, to whom it had a world of meaning.

Perhaps she did want a society in which her particular moral and religious beliefs were mirrored, and no others, instead of some plural, liberal mélange; a society in which her own cast of mind, her customs, way of life and obedience to God were established with full legal and constituted authority. But it wasn't as if anyone had asked her.

In Pakistan, England just wouldn't go away. Despite the Lahore lawyer, despite everything, England was very much on the minds of Pakistanis. Relics of the Raj were everywhere: buildings, monuments, Oxford accents, libraries full of English books and newspapers. Many Pakistanis had relatives in England; thousands of Pakistani families depended on money sent from England. Visiting a village, a man told me through an interpreter that when his three grandchildren visited from Bradford he had to hire an interpreter to speak to them. It was happening all the time – the closeness of the two societies, and the distance.

Although Pakistanis still wanted to escape to England, the old men in their clubs and the young eating their hamburgers took great pleasure in England's decline and decay. The great master was fallen. Now it was seen as strikebound, drug-ridden, riot-torn, inefficient, disunited, a society which had moved too suddenly from puritanism to hedonism and now loathed itself. And the Karachi wits liked to ask me when I thought the Americans would decide the British were ready for self-government.

Yet people like Rahman still clung to what they called British ideals, maintaining that it is a society's ideals, its conception of human progress, that define the level of its civilisation. They regretted, under the Islamisation, the repudiation of the values which they said were the only positive aspect of Britain's legacy to the sub-continent. These were: the idea of secular institutions based on reason, not revelation or scripture; the idea that there were no final solutions to human problems; and the idea that the health and vigour of a society was bound up with its ability to tolerate and express a plurality of views on all issues, and that these views would be welcomed.

The Black Album

Chapter Nine
(1995)

Shahid was about to pick up the phone in the hall and ring Deedee when Riaz announced it was prayer time.

In Karachi, at the urging of his cousins, Shahid had been to the mosque several times. While their parents would drink bootleg whisky and watch videos sent from England, Shahid's young relatives and their friends gathered in the house on Fridays before going to pray. The religious enthusiasm of the younger generation, and its links to strong political feeling, had surprised him. One time Shahid was demonstrating some yoga positions to one of his female cousins when her brother intervened violently, pulling his sister's ankles away from her ears. Yoga reminded him of 'those bloody Hindus'. This brother also refused to speak English, though it was, in that household, the first and common language; he asserted that Papa's generation, with their English accents, foreign degrees and British snobbery, assumed their own people were inferior. They should be forced to go into the villages and live among the peasants, as Gandhi had done.

At home Papa liked to say, when asked about his faith, 'Yes, I have a belief. It's called working until my arse aches!' Shahid and Chili had been taught little about religion. And on the occasions that Tipoo prayed in the house, Papa grumbled and complained, saying, why did he have to make such noises during repeats of his favourite programme, *The World at War*?

Now, though, Shahid was afraid his ignorance would place him in no man's land. These days everyone was insisting on their identity, coming out as a man, woman, gay, black, Jew – brandishing whichever features they could claim, as if without a tag they wouldn't be human. Shahid, too, wanted to belong to his people. But first he had to know them, their past and what they hoped for. Fortunately, Hat had been of great help. Several times he had interrupted his studies to visit Shahid's room with books; sitting beside him, he had, for hours, explained parts of

39

Islamic history, along with the essential beliefs. Then, clearing a space on the floor, he had demonstrated what to do.

While praying, Shahid had little notion of what to think, of what the cerebral concomitant to the actions should be. So, on his knees, he celebrated to himself the substantiality of the world, the fact of existence, the inexplicable phenomenon of life, art, humour and love itself – in murmured language, itself another sacred miracle. He accompanied this awe and wonder with suitable music, the 'Ode to Joy' from Beethoven's Ninth, for instance, which he hummed inaudibly.

Later that evening, the posse ate on the floor like guerrillas. They'd brought college work with them; but they'd come a long way, they were stirred up, there was much to be avenged: no books were opened.

Around eleven there was a bang on the door.

Armed, everyone rose, including Tahira and Nina. Pigeon-toed Riaz hefted a sort of scimitar, not looking as if he could hoist it over his shoulder, let alone crack apart a skinhead's skull. Chad was already in the hall and at the front door. He was bear-like, but he was a swift mover. Meaning business, he turned back his sleeves, revealing his thick arms. Before unbarring the entrance he bent forward to listen for a voice through the door.

To everyone's surprise Brownlow leapt into the living room, not only wearing sandals with white socks but speaking words. His bony forehead shone. Shahid was surprised by how white he looked, as if someone had neglected to turn the colour knob on the TV.

'Comrades!'

Apart from Riaz, they sat down again, relieved, disappointed.

'Good evening, comrades!' Brownlow declared. 'Any sign of the lunatics?'

'Not until you arrived,' Shahid murmured; the others smirked.

Riaz went to him. 'Not as yet,' he said. 'But we know that immoral people surround us. Dr Brownlow, we are so happy you received the message and were able to provide support.'

Brownlow opened his arms expansively, as if he wanted to embrace everyone. They were fighting in the same trench.

'Ghastly – this estate! What has been done to these people! Crimes against humanity. Important to visit wastelands regularly. Lest we forget. Seeing them, one understands a lot. It's obvious, not surprising –'

Finally disclosed, Brownlow's voice was a fruity sound that could hail a taxi across Knightsbridge, send waiters scurrying like kicked dogs, and instantaneously put down mutinous colonies without being strained. Whether barking, slurring, honking or ordering, the army, the City, the university, the country and England had honeyed every rotund syllable. Poor Andrew spoke from the very thing he hated. On the day of the revolution his first job would be to tear out his own tongue.

'I beg your pardon?' Riaz said amusedly, looking at him with some intensity.

Riaz was invariably courteous to Andrew, calling him Dr Brownlow and hanging on to his hand and cherishing it with little kiss-like pats, rather like the manager of an Indian restaurant greeting the mayor. At the same time Shahid knew by now that Riaz liked to have the advantage. His question, then, had a challenge in it. The group paid attention.

He continued: 'What is not surprising to you, Dr Brownlow, friend?'

But Brownlow was looking at Tahira with unmistakable lewdness; he was practically panting. He must have been on licensed premises a good few hours. Chad recognised it too, and stepped back as from a blowtorch. Tahira pinched the end of her nose and made a face.

Shahid felt queasy. Brownlow seemed gay tonight, and capable of mentioning seeing him at Deedee's house.

'Not surprising they're violent,' Brownlow said. 'This place. Living in ugliness. I've been wading around, you know, an hour or two in Hades, lost in the foul damp. I have seen giant dogs, sheer mournful walls, silos of misery. Sties. Breeding grounds of stink, these estates, for children. Ha! And race antipathy infecting everyone, passed on like Aids.'

Riaz continued to look at Brownlow and, as Chad said, when Riaz looked at someone they knew they were looked at. Riaz took a few paces; a speech was coming on. He began, 'But I could become fond of this estate.'

'Right. They've just decorated it up,' Chad growled.

Brownlow sensed a trap and became puzzled. 'Go on,' he said.

'I'll tell you, I would change places with the lucky buggers here tomorrow! Tomorrow!' Riaz's voice rose and rose. 'See how well fed they must be – they are so gross they can barely rouse their fat bottoms from the TV!' Everyone laughed, apart from Brownlow. 'They have housing, electricity, heating, TV, fridges, hospitals nearby! They can vote, participate politically or not. They are privileged indeed, are they not?'

'The people here can't oppose the corporations,' Brownlow said. 'Powerless, they are. Badly fed. Uneducated and unemployed. Can't make jobs from hope.'

Riaz went on: 'And do you think our brothers in the Third World, as you like to call most people other than you, have a fraction of this? Do our villages have electricity? Have you ever even seen a village?'

'An' he's not talking about Gloucestershire,' Chad muttered.

Brownlow said, 'In Soweto. Three months living with the people.'

'You will know, then,' Riaz said, 'that what I have said would be James Bond luxuries to the people there. They dream of having fridges, televisions, cookers! And are the people racist skinheads, car thieves, rapists? Have they desired to dominate the rest of the world? No, they are humble, good, hard-working people who love Allah!'

Shahid and the brothers murmured their assent. Brownlow must have regretted the moment he began to talk again. He was sensitive, and, with his belief in liberation, it must have cost him to take this from the man whose cause he supported.

He grimaced.

Shahid wondered if the others were as puzzled as he was. Here was someone who'd been granted breeding, privilege, education; his ancestors had circumnavigated the globe and ruled it. Shahid expected something more from all that had made him. At the same time he and the others couldn't help being pleased. The people who'd ruled them, and who still patronised and despised them, were not gods. Brought up to rule, to lead, now they were just another minority. Deedee had explained it to him. 'They send them away to school at seven where they do something awful to them. From this they never recover.'

Riaz politely indicated that he and Brownlow should sit together, at one side. Sadiq would unroll a clean Persian mat and bring a jug of water and tumblers. They could dispute in comfort.

Everyone was relaxing.

Shahid saw this as an opportunity to take out a novel. He hadn't read anything that day and missed the absorbed solitude. But even as he pulled a book from his bag he felt that somehow the others would disapprove of him reading on their night watch.

Instead, as Brownlow and Riaz began to talk, Shahid drew closer. When Riaz spoke at college or the mosque there was no debate, only soft questions. At the end, Riaz's group would slap his back, compliment him and push back enthusiasts.

Shahid felt he had passed the point when he could question Riaz about the fundamentals. Shahid frequently fell into anxiety about his lack of faith. Observing the mosque, in which all he saw were solid, material things, and looking along the line of brothers' faces upon which spirituality was taking place, he felt a failure. But he was afraid that enquiry would expose him to some sort of suspicion. He could at least discuss his doubts with Hat, who said not to worry, let it happen. And when Shahid did relax he grasped that faith, like love or creativity, could not be willed. This was an adventure in knowing. He had to follow the prescriptions and be patient. Understanding would surely follow; he would be blessed.

But now Brownlow, sitting cross-legged opposite Riaz, was reopening the wound of uncertainty.

'Often wished,' he was saying, addressing Shahid as well as Riaz, 'in my adult life, sometimes becoming desperate, that I could be religious. But read Bertrand Russell at fourteen. Expect you know him, don't you?'

'A bit,' Shahid said.

Brownlow wiggled his damp toes in his sandals. 'Deedee talk about him? Or does she only make you watch Prince videos?'

'She's a good teacher.'

Brownlow grunted and went on: 'Put the deity in his place, didn't he, Russell? Said that if He existed He would be a fool. Ha, ha, ha! Also said, quote, "The whole conception of God is a conception derived from the ancient Oriental despotisms." Good, eh? Since then often – me – felt abandoned in the universe. Atheism can be a terrible trouble, you should know. Having to invest the world with meaning. Would be marvellous to believe that soon after death by cancer one will slip – I mean, sip – grapes, melon and virgins in paradise. Paradise being like Venice. Without the smells or early closing. Heaven, surely, as someone said, was man's easiest invention.'

Shahid tried to smile. He wanted an alcoholic drink. He didn't know what had brought on such a sudden thirst – the fear or the company. Probably it was the talk of paradise.

Brownlow was becoming spirited.

'Wonderful on one's knees. Existing in an imaginary realm ruled by imaginary beings. Wonderful to have all rules of life delivered from on high. What to eat. How to wipe your bottom.' His bunched fingers were now inches from Riaz's nose, as if he were about to pluck it off and wipe his arse with it. 'How abhorrent too! The slave of superstition.'

Shahid balked. Brownlow was calling Riaz a slave of superstition! No one spoke to him like this! How would he react?

Brownlow went further: 'Magic realist tales from distant centuries! Bondage – surely you recognise bondage? And don't some of us weaklings prefer that to free will? Trading on infantile dependence – aren't you? D'you see?'

It must have been Brownlow's alcohol fumes which made Shahid yearn for the darkness of a pub. A pint of Speckled Hen, Southern Comfort, Heineken, Tennent's, Guinness, Becks, Pils, Bud – what lovely names, like those of the poets! His mouth was parched.

But Shahid struggled. He didn't want to be swung here and there by desire. Chili's excess and selfishness, for instance, disgusted him. Yet images of Brownlow's wife kept tempting him. At this moment, he could have been gripping her well-exercised calf, pressing her knee, cosseting his hand into her thigh and sliding inwards.

'Surely,' Brownlow said, 'surely the act of believing –'

'Believing as opposed to what?'

Riaz was not disconcerted by Brownlow's counter-attack, but looked on with the confidence of a chess player who has anticipated the next moves.

'As opposed to thinking. Of thinking without preconceptions and prejudices. Yes, surely the strain of believing something that can never be proven or shown to make logical sense must seem, for an intelligent man like you. To be. To be –' Brownlow searched for the least tendentious word. 'Dishonest! Yes. Dishonest!'

Brownlow wasn't restraining himself tonight.

Shahid examined the smile which was so frequently on Riaz's face. He was balding, he had a wart on his chin and one on his cheek; he could smell of sweat. But Shahid had taken it for granted that his smile indicated humour, a love of humanity, patience. Yet, if you looked closely, it was disdain. Riaz not only thought Brownlow was a fool, but thought him contemptible too.

'People must decide good and evil for themselves,' Brownlow said.

Riaz laughed. 'Man is the last person I would trust to such a task!'

Shahid stood up.

He would ask Chad if he could go for a walk. He could phone Deedee from the street. He wanted only to hear her voice now. But what if Chad refused him, which was quite likely? He'd be stuck then. Deedee would think he'd let her down.

Why did Shahid have to be scared of Chad? Chad had experienced unforgettable highs, and now he forced interminable restraint on himself. No wonder he was frantic and vexatious; everyday reality would always let him down. All the same, Chad was just another brother, albeit one who required forgiveness. Shahid would have to stand up for himself.

'Please excuse me,' Riaz was saying to Brownlow. 'But you are a little arrogant.' Brownlow chuckled. He was enjoying the argument. 'Your liberal beliefs belong to a minority who live in northern Europe. Yet you think moral superiority over the rest of mankind is a fact. You want to dominate others with your particular morality, which has – as you also well know – gone hand-in-hand with fascist imperialism.' Here Riaz leaned towards Brownlow. 'This is why we have to guard against the hypocritical and smug intellectual atmosphere of Western civilisation.'

Brownlow dabbed sweat from his forehead and smiled. His eyes scattered about. He didn't know where to begin. He took a breath.

That atmosphere you deprecate. With reason. But this civilisation has also brought us this –'

'Dr Brownlow, tell us what it has brought us,' Shahid said.

'Good, Tariq. A student with curiosity. Let's think.' On his fingers he counted them off. 'Literature, painting, architecture, psychoanalysis, science, journalism, music, a stable political culture, organised sport – at a pretty high level. And all this has gone hand-in-hand with something significant. That is: critical enquiry into the nature of truth. It talks of proof and demonstration.'

Riaz said slyly, 'Like Marx's famous dialectic, you mean?'

For a moment Brownlow halted. He continued: 'And steely questions. Without flinching. Questions and ideas. Ideas being the enemy of religion.'

'So much the worse for the ideas,' Riaz said, with a snort.

They both looked at him. It was an argument Shahid felt barely able to participate in. He cursed himself for being inarticulate and ignorant, just as he had been when Chad had asked him why he loved literature. But it was a spur, too: he would have to study, read more and think, combining facts and arguments in ways that fitted the world as he saw it.

Shahid glanced across at Chad. He got up and moved to the door.

'Just popping out,' he whispered to Riaz, leaving the room as quickly as he could.

In the hall he picked up the phone and dialled quickly.

'I'm scared,' Tahira said. 'Aren't you?'

He nodded. She wasn't going to move away. When he heard Deedee's voice he replaced the receiver.

'I'll just be back,' he said to Tahira, pulling the bolts, turning the keys and releasing the chain on the door.

'Where are you going?'

'One of us should case the neighbourhood. Check the layout and all.'

'Good. But not alone. Let me come.'

'No, no.'

'I'm really not afraid.'

'But I'd be afraid for you.'

Shahid slipped out of the door.

It took him a while to get off the estate. He doubted that he'd find a phone even then. Fine drizzle fell, it was like walking through a cloud. He smelled the rain; it had been some time, in this city, since he had smelled anything so fresh. It was humid too and the pavements steamed, like a music video. He wouldn't find his way back now. Nor would he be able to find his way home.

This area was notorious for racists. He began to jog, and then to run. Under a sombre railway bridge he spotted the taxi driver who'd brought them, dropping off a customer. Shahid went up to him. He remembered Shahid and led him into the taxi office. Unearthly noises were coming from the back room. The man extended his hand, barring Shahid's way. He glanced around the door and saw the drivers playing cards while watching a porn video.

They let him call her from the front office. At last he got through.

'Where have you been? I've been waiting here for two hours! Couldn't you have called before? D'you think a woman would do such a thing to a man?'

Before the humiliation and annoyance in Deedee's voice could affect him, he explained that he'd been called out on urgent brother business. A year ago Sadiq's fifteen-year-old brother had had his skull crushed by a dozen youths. This particular duty had to be taken seriously.

She wouldn't accept it. It was as if she blamed him for the disappointments other men had given her, and for the hope which he, evidently, had stirred in her.

'Sorry, sorry, sorry,' he repeated. 'What could I do?'

While they talked he saw, from the window, a boy standing outside, the red spot of his cigarette glowing through the sticky drizzle. Probably he was waiting for a cab. Then the boy turned, looked right at Shahid and nodded.

'Even now,' Shahid said, 'there are racists outside, waiting for me.'

She told him to get a cab – which she would pay for – and come over now, at least for a drink. She despised herself for asking this, he could tell.

'But I can't,' he said. 'Not tonight.'

'When, then?'

'Soon, soon. I'll ring you.'

'Promise?'

'Yes.'

He got off the phone as quickly as he could, and asked the driver to take him back to the flat. When they left the office the kid had gone.

The gang sat up all night, sleeping on the floor in shifts. The next morning those who had lectures and college work left, and were replaced by others. Shahid, who had a clear day, didn't get away until that afternoon, and by then a bomb had exploded on the main concourse of Victoria Station.

The Road Exactly

Introduction to the screenplay of
My Son the Fanatic
(1998)

The idea for *My Son the Fanatic*, as for *The Black Album*, was provided by my thinking about the fatwa against Salman Rushdie, announced in February 1989. At that time various politicians, thinkers and artists spoke out in the media about this extraordinary intellectual terror. A surprising number of statements were fatuous and an excuse for abuse and prejudice; some expressed genuine outrage, and most were confused but comfortingly liberal. The attack on Rushdie certainly made people think afresh about the point and place of literature, about what stories were for, and about their relation to dissent.

But few commentators noticed that the objections to *The Satanic Verses* represented another kind of protest. In Britain many young Asians were turning to Islam, and some to a particularly extreme form, often called fundamentalism. Most of these young people were from Muslim families, of course, but usually families in which the practice of religion, in a country to which their families had come to make a new life, had fallen into disuse.

It perplexed me that young people, brought up in secular Britain, would turn to a form of belief that denied them the pleasures of the society in which they lived. Islam was a particularly firm way of saying 'no' to all sorts of things. Young people's lives are, for a lot of the time, devoted to pleasure: the pleasure of sex and music, of clubbing, friendship, and the important pleasure of moving away from one's parents to develop one's own ideas. Why was it important that this group kept pleasure at a distance? Why did they wish to maintain such a tantalising relation to their own enjoyment, keeping it so fervently in mind, only to deny it? Or was this puritanism a kind of rebellion, a brave refusal of the order of the age – an over-sexualised but sterile society? Were these young Muslims people who dared to try nothing? Whatever the reason, there was, clearly, a future in illusion; not only that, illusions were once more becoming a sound investment. But what sort of future did they require?

To the surprise of most of us, it sometimes seems that we are living in a new theocratic age. I imagined that the sixties, with its penchant for seeing through things and pulling them apart with laughter and questions, had cleared that old church stuff away. But the sixties, in the West, with its whimsy and drugged credulity, also helped finish off the Enlightenment. It was during the sixties that weird cults, superstitious groups, new agers, strange therapists, seers, gurus and leaders of all kinds came to prominence. This need for belief and the establishment of new idols was often innocuous – a mixture of the American idea of self-fulfilment and the Greek notion of fully extended man, vitiated by a good dose of ordinary repression.

But the kind of religion favoured by the young Muslims was particularly strict and frequently authoritarian. An old religion was being put to a new use, and it was that use which interested me. I wondered constantly why people would wish to give so much of their own autonomy, the precious freedom of their own minds, to others – to Maulvis, and to the Koran. After all, the young people I met were not stupid; many were very intelligent. But they put a lot of effort into the fashioning of a retributive God to which to submit.

Clearly, where there is a 'crisis of authority', when, it seems, people aren't certain of anything because ancient hierarchies have been brought down, the answer is to create a particularly strict authority, where troubling questions cannot be admitted. 'There's too much freedom,' one of the young men, Ali, kept saying to me, someone who'd always thought that freedom was something you couldn't get enough of. This intrigued me.

Ali worked for a well-known supermarket chain, stacking shelves, though he had a degree. It was boring work; to get anywhere you had to grovel, or go to the bar and drink and exchange unpleasant banter. Sometimes you had to shake hands with women. Anyhow, the Asians didn't get promoted. A reason for this, he liked to muse, was that the major businesses were run by Jews. He applied for jobs all the time, but never got them. I couldn't see why this was so. He was certainly courteous. He

brought me presents: a tie, mangos, the Koran. He was intellectually curious too, and liked showing me the new books he
bought constantly. He knew a great deal about the history and
politics of the Middle East, about which, he claimed, the
average Westerner knew little. Ali knew the West, but the West
didn't know him except through tendentious media images. The
West, therefore, had no idea of its own arrogance, and was certainly not concerned about the extent to which it had no interest
in anything outside itself.

Just when I thought there wasn't much Ali and I could argue
about, he would say he didn't disapprove of the killings of
journalists – and others – in Algeria. They were 'enemies'; he
took it for granted that they were guilty. Perhaps, for him, the
fact they were murdered made them guilty. During such
conversations he liked to quote Malcolm X's phrase at me:
'By any means necessary', a modern motto of liberation thus
becoming a tool of tyranny. I couldn't recall the context in
which Malcolm X's phrase was first used, but it was clear that it
could be applied to anything; its meaning had become unstable.
These days not even language would hold still. Indeed, Ali
himself could be called a 'fundamentalist', a word newly minted
to mean a fanatical Muslim. It was a word he even applied to
himself. At the same time he complained about Muslims being
portrayed in the press as 'terrorists' and 'fanatics'. This argument, which had begun because of a book, continued to be about
language and about what words mean, as much as anything.

The 'West' was a word, like liberalism, for anything bad. The
West's freedom made him feel unsafe. If there was too much
freedom you had to make less of it. I asked him about the diffi-
culty of giving up things. He had been keen on clubs; he'd had
an affair with a married woman. Renunciation made him feel
strong, he said, while giving in made him feel weak. Wasn't the
West full of addicts?

The West, therefore, was a place full of things he disliked – or
where he liked to put them; and where people gave in to things
he disapproved of. He gave me a flyer for a Muslim rally in

Trafalgar Square that stated, 'Endemic crime, homosexuality, poverty, family breakdown, drug and alcohol abuse show Western freedom and democracy just aren't working.' Because of this, Ali and his friends would never bring up their children here. But it also meant that he hated his own background, the forces that influenced him and the place he lived in.

His attitude kept reminding me of something I had heard before. Finally I realised it took me back to a paragraph in Czeslaw Milosz's The *Captive Mind* (Milosz is here referring to Eastern European communist intellectuals): 'The official order is to evince the greatest horror of the West. Everything is evil there: trains are late, stores are empty, no one has money, people are poorly dressed, the highly praised technology is worthless. If you hear the name of a Western writer, painter or composer, you must scoff sarcastically, for to fight against "cosmopolitanism" is one of the basic duties of a citizen.'

Constraint could be a bulwark against a self that was always in danger of dissolving in the face of too much choice, opportunity and desire. By opposing that which continually changes around us, by denying those things we might want, we keep ourselves together. In the face of such decadent possibilities and corrupt pleasures – or where there is the fear of what free or disobedient people might do – Islam would provide the necessary deprivation and could attenuate the repertoire of possible selves.

Open the Koran on almost any page and there is a threat. 'We have adorned the lowest heaven with lamps, missiles for pelting devils. We have prepared a scourge of flames for these, and the scourge of Hell for unbelievers: an evil fate!'

There is, then, sufficient regulation and punishment available. Without harsh constraint things might get out of hand, particularly in the postmodern world, where no one knows anything for sure. And so, against the 'corruption' of the West to which so many had innocently travelled, a new authority could be posited – that of Islam and, in particular, those who spoke for it. Without the revolutionary or opposing idea of Purity there wouldn't be those who knew what it was and could tell us when it had been violated. These men – and they were always men – became very powerful. The young invested a lot of authority in them.

Edward Said wrote: 'There are now immigrant communities in Europe from the former colonial territories to whom the ideas of "France" and "Britain" and "Germany" as constituted during the period between 1800 and 1950 simply excludes them.'

It must not be forgotten, therefore, that the backgrounds to the lives of these young people includes colonialism – being made to feel inferior in your own country. And then, in Britain, racism; again, being made to feel inferior in your own country. My father's generation came to Britain full of hope and expectation. It would be an adventure, it would be difficult, but it would be worth it.

However, the settling in, with all the compromises and losses that that implies, has been more complicated and taken longer than anyone could imagine. Yet all along it was taken for granted that 'belonging', which means, in a sense, not having to notice where you are, and, more importantly, not being seen as different, would happen eventually. Where it hasn't, there is, in the children and grandchildren of the great post-war wave of immigrants, considerable anger and disillusionment. With some exceptions, Asians are still at the bottom of the pile; more likely to suffer from unemployment, poor housing, discrimination and ill-health. In a sense it hasn't worked out. The 'West' was a dream that didn't come true. But one cannot go home again. One is stuck.

Clearly this affects people in different ways. But without a doubt it is constraining, limiting, degrading, to be a victim in your own country. If you feel excluded it might be tempting to exclude others. The fundamentalists liked to reject the usual liberal pieties, sometimes for histrionic reasons. But their enemies – gays, Jews, the media, unsubmissive women, writers – were important to them. Their idea of themselves was based, like the MCC, or like any provincial snob, on whom they excluded. Not only that, the central tenets of the West – democracy, pluralism, tolerance, which many people in Islamic countries, Muslim and non-Muslim alike, are struggling for – could be treated as a joke. For those whose lives had been negated by colonialism and racism such notions could only seem a luxury and of no benefit to them; they were a kind of hypocrisy.

Therefore, during our conversations Ali continuously argued that there are no such things as freedom or democracy, or that those abstractions were only real for a small group. For him, if they didn't exist in the purest possible form, they didn't exist at all. Milosz might call Ali's attitude, with some sadness, 'disappointed love', and it was a disappointment that seemed to attach itself to everything. Which isn't to say there wasn't hope too. For instance, he believed that when the existing corrupt rulers of Muslim countries were swept away, they would be replaced by 'true' Muslims, benign in every way, who would work for the benefit of the people, according to the word of God. If the present was unsatisfactory and impossible to live in, as it always would be for him, there was the perfect future, which would, probably, safely remain the future – the best place for it, for his purposes.

Fundamentalism provides security. For the fundamentalist, as for all reactionaries, everything has been decided. Truth has been agreed and nothing must change. For serene liberals, on the other hand, the consolations of knowing seem less satisfying than the pleasures of puzzlement, and of wanting to discover for oneself. But the feeling that one cannot know everything, that there will always be maddening and live questions about who one is and how it is possible to make a life with other people who don't accept one, can be devastating. Perhaps it is only for so long that one can live with that kind of puzzlement. Rationalists have always underestimated the need people have for belief. Enlightenment values – rationalism, tolerance, scepticism – don't get you through a dreadful night; they don't provide spiritual comfort or community or solidarity. Fundamentalist Islam could do this in a country that was supposed to be home but which could, from day to day, seem alien.

Muslim fundamentalism has always seemed to me to be profoundly wrong, unnecessarily restrictive and frequently cruel. But there are reasons for its revival that are comprehensible. It is this that has made me want to look at it not only in terms of ideas, but in stories, in character, in terms of what people do. For a writer there cannot be just one story, a story to end all stories in which everything is said, but as many stories as one wants, serving all sorts of purposes and sometimes none at all. The primary object, though, is to provide pleasure of different kinds. And one must remember that perhaps the greatest book of all, and certainly one of the most pleasurable, *The One Thousand and One Nights* is, like the Koran, written in Arabic. This creativity, the making of something that didn't exist before, the vigour and stretch of a living imagination, is a human affirmation of another kind, and a necessary and important form of self-examination. Without it our humanity is diminished.

My Son the Fanatic

A story
(1997)

Surreptitiously the father began going into his son's bedroom. He would sit there for hours, rousing himself only to seek clues. What bewildered him was that Ali was getting tidier. Instead of the usual tangle of clothes, books, cricket bats, video games, the room was becoming neat and ordered; spaces began appearing where before there had been only mess.

Initially Parvez had been pleased: his son was outgrowing his teenage attitudes. But one day, beside the dustbin, Parvez found a torn bag which contained not only old toys, but computer discs, video tapes, new books and fashionable clothes the boy had bought just a few months before. Also without explanation, Ali had parted from the English girlfriend who used to come often to the house. His old friends had stopped ringing.

For reasons he didn't himself understand, Parvez wasn't able to bring up the subject of Ali's unusual behaviour. He was aware that he had become slightly afraid of his son, who, alongside his silences, was developing a sharp tongue. One remark Parvez did make, 'You don't play your guitar any more,' elicited the mysterious but conclusive reply, 'There are more important things to be done.'

Yet Parvez felt his son's eccentricity as an injustice. He had always been aware of the pitfalls which other men's sons had fallen into in England. And so, for Ali, he had worked long hours and spent a lot of money paying for his education as an accountant. He had bought him good suits, all the books he required and a computer. And now the boy was throwing his possessions out!

The TV, video and sound system followed the guitar. Soon the room was practically bare. Even the unhappy walls bore marks where Ali's pictures had been removed.

Parvez couldn't sleep; he went more to the whisky bottle, even when he was at work. He realised it was imperative to discuss the matter with someone sympathetic.

Parvez had been a taxi driver for twenty years. Half that time he'd worked for the same firm. Like him, most of the other drivers were Punjabis. They preferred to work at night, the roads wereaclearer and the money better. They slept during the day, avoiding their wives. Together they led almost a boy's life in the cabbies' office, playing cards and practical jokes, exchanging lewd stories, eating together and discussing politics and their problems.

But Parvez had been unable to bring this subject up with his friends. He was too ashamed. And he was afraid, too, that they would blame him for the wrong turning his boy had taken, just as he had blamed other fathers whose sons had taken to running around with bad girls, truanting from school and joining gangs.

For years Parvez had boasted to the other men about how Ali excelled at cricket, swimming and football, and how attentive a scholar he was, getting straight 'A's in most subjects. Was it asking too much for Ali to get a good job now, marry the right girl and start a family? Once this happened, Parvez would be happy. His dreams of doing well in England would have come true. Where had he gone wrong?

But one night, sitting in the taxi office on busted chairs with his two closest friends watching a Sylvester Stallone film, he broke his silence.

'I can't understand it!' he burst out. 'Everything is going from his room. And I can't talk to him any more. We were not father and son – we were brothers! Where has he gone? Why is he torturing me!'

And Parvez put his head in his hands.

Even as he poured out his account the men shook their heads and gave one another knowing glances. From their grave looks Parvez realised they understood the situation.

'Tell me what is happening!' he demanded.

The reply was almost triumphant. They had guessed something was going wrong. Now it was clear. Ali was taking drugs and selling his possessions to pay for them. That was why his bedroom was emptying.

'What must I do, then?'

Parvez's friends instructed him to watch Ali scrupulously and then be severe with him, before the boy went mad, overdosed or murdered someone.

Parvez staggered out into the early morning air, terrified they were right. His boy – the drug-addict killer!

To his relief he found Bettina sitting in his car.

Usually the last customers of the night were local 'brasses' or prostitutes. The taxi drivers knew them well, often driving them to liaisons. At the end of the girls' shifts, the men would ferry them home, though sometimes the women would join them for a drinking session in the office. Occasionally the drivers would go with the girls. 'A ride in exchange for a ride,' it was called.

Bettina had known Parvez for three years. She lived outside the town and on the long drive home, when she sat not in the passenger seat but beside him. Parvez had talked to her about his life and hopes, just as she talked about hers. They saw each other most nights.

He could talk to her about things he'd never be able to discuss with his own wife. Bettina, in turn, always reported on her night's activities. He liked to know where she was and with whom. Once he had rescued her from a violent client, and since then they had come to care for one another.

Though Bettina had never met the boy, she heard about Ali continually. That late night, when he told Bettina that he suspected Ali was on drugs, she judged neither the boy nor his father, but became businesslike and told him what to watch for.

'It's all in the eyes,' she said. They might be bloodshot; the pupils might be dilated; he might look tired. He could be liable to sweats, or sudden mood changes. 'Okay?'

Parvez began his vigil gratefully. Now he knew what the problem might be, he felt better. And surely, he figured, things couldn't have gone too far? With Bettina's help he would soon sort it out.

He watched each mouthful the boy took. He sat beside him at every opportunity and looked into his eyes. When he could he took the boy's hand, checking his temperature. If the boy wasn't at home Parvez was active, looking under the carpet, in his drawers, behind the empty wardrobe, sniffing, inspecting, probing. He knew what to look for: Bettina had drawn pictures of capsules, syringes, pills, powders, rocks.

Every night she waited to hear news of what he'd witnessed.

After a few days of constant observation, Parvez was able to report that although the boy had given up sports, he seemed healthy, with clear eyes. He didn't, as his father expected, flinch guiltily from his gaze. In fact the boy's mood was alert and steady in this sense: as well as being sullen, he was very watchful. He returned his father's long looks with more than a hint of criticism, of reproach even, so much so that Parvez began to feel that it was he who was in the wrong and not the boy!

'And there's nothing else physically different?' Bettina asked.

'No!' Parvez thought for a moment. 'But he is growing a beard.'

One night, after sitting with Bettina in an all-night coffee shop, Parvez came home particularly late. Reluctantly he and Bettina had abandoned their only explanation, the drug theory, for Parvez had found nothing resembling any drug in Ali's room. Besides, Ali wasn't selling his belongings. He threw them out, gave them away or donated them to charity shops.

Standing in the hall, Parvez heard his boy's alarm clock go off. Parvez hurried into his bedroom where his wife was still awake, sewing in bed. He ordered her to sit down and keep quiet, though she had neither stood up nor said a word. From this post, and with her watching him curiously, he observed his son through the crack in the door.

The boy went into the bathroom to wash. When he returned to his room Parvez sprang across the hall and set his ear at Ali's door. A muttering sound came from within. Parvez was puzzled but relieved.

Once this clue had been established, Parvez watched him at other times. The boy was praying. Without fail, when he was at home, he prayed five times a day.

Parvez had grown up in Lahore, where all the boys had been taught the Koran. To stop him falling asleep when he studied, the Maulvis had attached a piece of string to the ceiling and tied it to Parvez's hair, so that if his head fell forward he would instantly awake. After this indignity Parvez had avoided all religions. Not that the other taxi drivers had more respect. In fact they made jokes about the local mullahs walking around with their caps and beards, thinking they could tell people how to live, while their eyes roved over the boys and girls in their care.

Parvez described to Bettina what he had discovered. He informed the men in the taxi office. The friends, who had been so curious before, now became oddly silent. They could hardly condemn the boy for his devotions.

Parvez decided to take a night off and go out with the boy. They could talk things over. He wanted to hear how things were going at college; he wanted to tell him stories about their family in Pakistan. More than anything he yearned to understand how Ali had discovered the 'spiritual dimension', as Bettina described it.

To Parvez's surprise, the boy refused to accompany him. He claimed he had an appointment. Parvez had to insist that no appointment could be more important than that of a son with his father.

The next day, Parvez went immediately to the street where Bettina stood in the rain wearing high heels, a short skirt and a long mac on top, which she would open hopefully at passing cars.

'Get in, get in!' he said.

They drove out across the moors and parked at the spot where on better days, with a view unimpeded for many miles by nothing but wild deer and horses, they'd lie back, with their eyes half closed, saying 'This is the life.' This time Parvez was trembling. Bettina put her arms around him.

'What's happened?'

'I've just had the worst experience of my life.'

As Bettina rubbed his head Parvez told her that the previous evening he and Ali had gone to a restaurant. As they studied the menu, the waiter, whom Parvez knew, brought him his usual whisky and water. Parvez had been so nervous he had even prepared a question. He was going to ask Ali if he was worried about his imminent exams. But first, wanting to relax, he loosened his tie, crunched a popadom and took a long drink.

Before Parvez could speak, Ali made a face.

'Don't you know it's wrong to drink alcohol?' he said.

'He spoke to me very harshly,' Parvez told Bettina. 'I was about to castigate the boy for being insolent, but managed to control myself.'

He had explained patiently to Ali that for years he had worked more than ten hours a day, that he had few enjoyments or hobbies and never went on holiday. Surely it wasn't a crime to have a drink when he wanted one?

'But it is forbidden,' the boy said.

Parvez shrugged. 'I know.'

'And so is gambling, isn't it?'

'Yes. But surely we are only human?'

Each time Parvez took a drink, the boy winced, or made a fastidious face as an accompaniment. This made Parvez drink more quickly. The waiter, wanting to please his friend, brought another glass of whisky. Parvez knew he was getting drunk, but he couldn't stop himself. Ali had a horrible look on his face, full of disgust and censure. It was as if he hated his father.

Halfway through the meal Parvez suddenly lost his temper and threw a plate on the floor. He had felt like ripping the cloth from the table, but the waiters and other customers were staring at him. Yet he wouldn't stand for his own son telling him the difference between right and wrong. He knew he wasn't a bad man. He had a conscience. There were a few things of which he was ashamed, but on the whole he had lived a decent life.

When have I had time to be wicked?' he asked Ali.

In a low monotonous voice the boy explained that Parvez had not, in fact, lived a good life. He had broken countless rules of the Koran.

'For instance?' Parvez demanded.

Ali hadn't needed time to think. As if he had been waiting for this moment, he asked his father if he didn't relish pork pies.

'Well . . .'

Parvez couldn't deny that he loved crispy bacon smothered with mushrooms and mustard and sandwiched between slices of fried bread. In fact he ate this for breakfast every morning.

Ali then reminded Parvez that he had ordered his own wife to cook pork sausages, saying to her, 'You're not in the village now, this is England. We have to fit in!'

Parvez was so annoyed and perplexed by this attack that he called for more drink.

'The problem is this,' the boy said. He leaned across the table. For the first time that night his eyes were alive. 'You are too implicated in Western civilisation.'

Parvez burped; he thought he was going to choke. 'Implicated!' he said. 'But we live here!'

'The Western materialists hate us,' Ali said. 'Papa, how can you love something which hates you?'

'What is the answer then?' Parvez said miserably. 'According to you?'

Ali addressed his father fluently, as if Parvez were a rowdy crowd that had to be quelled and convinced. The Law of Islam would rule the world; the skin of the infidel would burn off again and again; the Jews and Christers would be routed. The West was a sink of hypocrites, adulterers, homosexuals, drug-takers and prostitutes.

As Ali talked, Parvez looked out of the window as if to check that they were still in London.

'My people have taken enough. If the persecution doesn't stop there will be *jihad*. I, and millions of others, will gladly give our lives for the cause.'

'But why, why?' Parvez said.

'For us the reward will be in paradise.'

'Paradise!'

Finally, as Parvez's eyes filled with tears, the boy urged him to mend his ways.

'How is that possible?' Parvez asked.

'Pray,' Ali said. 'Pray beside me.'

Parvez called for the bill and ushered his boy out of the restaurant as soon as he was able. He couldn't take any more. Ali sounded as if he'd swallowed someone else's voice.

On the way home the boy sat in the back of the taxi, as if he were a customer.

'What has made you like this?' Parvez asked him, afraid that somehow he was to blame for all this. 'Is there a particular event which has influenced you?'

'Living in this country.'

'But I love England,' Parvez said, watching his boy in the mirror. 'They let you do almost anything here.'

'That is the problem,' he replied.

For the first time in years Parvez couldn't see straight. He knocked the side of the car against a lorry, ripping off the wing mirror. They were lucky not to have been stopped by the police: Parvez would have lost his licence and therefore his job.

Getting out of the car back at the house, Parvez stumbled and fell in the mad, scraping his hands and ripping his trousers. He managed to haul himself up. The boy didn't even offer him his hand.

Parvez told Bettina he was now willing to pray, if that was what the boy wanted, if that would dislodge the pitiless look from his eyes.

'But what I object to,' he said, 'is being told by my own son that I am going to hell!'

What finished Parvez off was that the boy had said he was giving up accountancy. When Parvez had asked why, Ali had said sarcastically that it was obvious.

'Western education cultivates an anti-religious attitude.'

And, according to Ali, in the world of accountants it was usual to meet women, drink alcohol and practise usury.

'But it's well-paid work,' Parvez argued. 'For years you've been preparing!'

Ali said he was going to begin to work in prisons, with poor Muslims who were struggling to maintain their purity in the face of corruption. Finally, at the end of the evening, as Ali was going to bed, he had asked his father why he didn't have a beard, or at least a moustache.

'I feel as if I've lost my son,' Parvez told Bettina. 'I can't bear to be looked at as if I'm a criminal. I've decided what to do.'

'What is it?'

'I'm going to tell him to pick up his prayer mat and get out of my house. It will be the hardest thing I've ever done, but tonight I'm going to do it.'

'But you mustn't give up on him,' said Bettina. 'Many young people fall into cults and superstitious groups. It doesn't mean they'll always feel the same way.'

She said Parvez had to stick by his boy, giving him support, until he came through.

Parvez was persuaded that she was right, even though he didn't feel like giving his son more love when he had hardly been thanked for all he had already given.

Nevertheless, Parvez tried to endure his son's looks and reproaches. He attempted to make conversation about his beliefs. But if Parvez ventured any criticism, Ali always had a brusque reply. On one occasion Ali accused Parvez of 'grovelling' to the whites; in contrast, he explained, he was not 'inferior'; there was more to the world than the West, though the West always thought it was best.

'How is it you know that?' Parvez said. 'Seeing as you've never left England?'

Ali replied with a look of contempt.

One night, having ensured there was no alcohol on his breath, Parvez sat down at the kitchen table with Ali. He hoped Ali would compliment him on the beard he was growing but Ali didn't appear to notice.

The previous day Parvez had been telling Bettina that he thought people in the West sometimes felt inwardly empty and that people needed a philosophy to live by.

'Yes,' said Bettina. 'That's the answer. You must tell him what your philosophy of life is. Then he will understand that there are other beliefs.'

After some fatiguing consideration, Parvez was ready to begin. The boy watched him as if he expected nothing.

Haltingly Parvez said that people had to treat one another with respect, particularly children their parents. This did seem, for a moment, to affect the boy. Heartened, Parvez continued. In his view this life was all there was and when you died you rotted in the earth. 'Grass and flowers will grow out of me, but something of me will live on –'

'How?'

'In other people. I will continue – in you.' At this the boy appeared a little distressed. 'And your grandchildren,' Parvez added for good measure. 'But while I am here on earth I want to make the best of it. And I want you to, as well!'

'What d'you mean by "make the best of it"?' asked the boy.

'Well,' said Parvez. 'For a start . . . you should enjoy yourself. Yes. Enjoy yourself without hurting others.'

Ali said that enjoyment was a 'bottomless pit'.

'But I don't mean enjoyment like that!' said Parvez. 'I mean the beauty of living!'

'All over the world our people are oppressed,' was the boy's reply.

'I know,' Parvez replied, not entirely sure who 'our people' were, 'but still – life is for living!'

Ali said, 'Real morality has existed for hundreds of years. Around the world millions and millions of people share my beliefs. Are you saying you are right and they are all wrong?'

Ali looked at his father with such aggressive confidence that Parvez could say no more.

One evening Bettina was sitting in Parvez's car, after visiting a client, when they passed a boy on the street.

'That's my son,' Parvez said suddenly. They were on the other side of town, in a poor district, where there were two mosques. Parvez set his face hard.

Bettina turned to watch him. 'Slow down then, slow down!' she said. 'He's good-looking. Reminds me of you. But with a more determined face. Please, can't we stop?'

'What for?'

'I'd like to talk to him.'

Parvez turned the cab round and stopped beside the boy.

'Coming home?' Parvez asked. 'It's quite a way.'

The sullen boy shrugged and got into the back seat. Bettina sat in the front. Parvez became aware of Bettina's short skirt, gaudy rings and ice-blue eye shadow. He became conscious that the smell of her perfume, which he loved, filled the cab. He opened the window.

While Parvez drove as fast as he could, Bettina said gently to Ali, 'Where have you been?'

'The mosque,' he said.

'And how are you getting on at college? Are you working hard?'

'Who are you to ask me these questions?' he said, looking out of the window. Then they hit bad traffic and the car came to a standstill.

By now Bettina had inadvertently laid her hand on Parvez's shoulder. She said, 'Your father, who is a good man, is very worried about you. You know he loves you more than his own life.'

'You say he loves me,' the boy said.

'Yes!' said Bettina.

'Then why is he letting a woman like you touch him like that?'

If Bettina looked at the boy in anger, he looked back at her with twice as much cold fury.

She said, 'What kind of woman am I that deserves to be spoken to like that?'

'You know,' he said. 'Now let me out.'

'Never,' Parvez replied.

'Don't worry, I'm getting out,' Bettina said.

'No, don't!' said Parvez. But even as the car moved she opened the door, threw herself out and ran away across the road. Parvez shouted after her several times, but she had gone.

Parvez took Ali back to the house, saying nothing more to him. Ali went straight to his room. Parvez was unable to read the paper, watch television or even sit down. He kept pouring himself drinks.

At last he went upstairs and paced up and down outside Ali's room. When, finally, he opened the door, Ali was praying. The boy didn't even glance his way.

Parvez kicked him over. Then he dragged the boy up by his shirt and hit him. The boy fell back. Parvez hit him again. The boy's face was bloody. Parvez was panting. He knew that the boy was unreachable, but he struck him nonetheless. The boy neither covered himself nor retaliated; there was no fear in his eyes. He only said, through his split lip: 'So who's the fanatic now?'

Bradford

from
Granta 20
(Winter 1986)

Batley is outside Bradford, on the way to Leeds. It is a small town surrounded by countryside and hills. The view from the hill into the valley and then up into the hills was exquisite. In the town there was a large Asian community. The Zakariya Girls School had actually been started two years ago as a 'pirate' school, not having received approval from the Department of Education until an extension was built. Now it was finished. And today it became the first high school of its kind – an Islamic school for girls – to be officially registered under the Education Act. As a pirate school it had been a large, overcrowded old house on the top of a hill. Now, outside, was a new two-storey building. It was spacious, clean, modern.

I went in and looked around. Most of the books were on the Koran or Islam, on prayer or on the prophet Mohammed. The walls were covered with verses from the Koran. And despite its being a girls' school there were no girls there and no Asian women, just the men and lots of little boys in green, blue and brown caps, running about.

The idea for the school had been the pop star Cat Stevens's, and he had raised most of the money for it privately, it was said, from Saudi Arabia. Stevens, who had changed his name to Yusaf Islam, was quoted as saying that he had tried everything, running the gamut of international novelties to find spiritual satisfaction: materialism, sex, drugs, Buddhism, Christianity and finally Islam. I wondered if it was entirely arbitrary that he'd ended with Islam or whether perhaps today, the circumstances being slightly different, we could as easily have been at the opening of a Buddhist school.

Yusaf Islam was not at the school but his assistant, Ibrahim, was. Ibrahim was the white Muslim in the white robes with the white turban who spoke earlier. There was supposed to be a press conference, but nothing was happening; everything was disorganised. Ibrahim came and sat beside me. I asked him if he'd talk about the school. He was, he said, very keen; the school had been the result of so much effort and organisation, so much goodness. I looked at him. He seemed preternaturally good and calm.

Ibrahim was from Newcastle, and had a long ginger beard. (I remembered someone saying to me in Pakistan that the only growth industry in Islamic countries was in human hair on the face.) Ibrahim's epiphany had occurred on a trip to South Africa. There, seeing black and white men praying together in a mosque, he decided to convert to Islam.

He told me about the way the school worked. The human face, for instance, or the face of any animate being, could not be represented at the school. And dancing would not be encouraged, nor the playing of musical instruments. Surely, he said, looking at me, his face full of conviction, the human voice was expressive enough? When I said this would probably rule out the possibility of the girls taking either Art or Music O-Levels, he nodded sadly and admitted that it would.

And modern literature? I asked.

He nodded sadly again and said it would be studied 'in a critical light'.

I said I was glad to hear it. But what about science?

That was to be studied in a critical light too, since – and here he took a deep breath – he didn't accept Darwinism or any theory of evolution because, well, because the presence of monkeys who hadn't changed into men disproved it all.

I took another close look at him. He obviously believed these things. But why was he being so apologetic?

As I walked back down the hill I thought about the issues raised by the Zakariya Girls School. There were times, I thought, when to be accommodating you had to bend over backwards so far that you fell over. Since the mid-1960s the English liberal has seen the traditional hierarchies and divisions of British life challenged, if not destroyed. Assumptions of irrevocable, useful and moral differences – between classes, men and women, gays and straights, older and younger people, developed and under-developed societies – had changed for good. The commonly made distinction between 'higher' and 'lower' cultures had become suspect. It had become questionable philosophically to apply criteria of judgement available in one society to events in another: there could not be any independent or bridging method of evaluation. And it followed that we should be able, as a broad, humane and pluralistic society, to sustain a wide range of disparate groups living in their own way. And if one of these groups wanted *halal* meat, Islamic schools, anti-Darwinism and an intimate knowledge of the Koran for its girls, so be it. As it was, there had been Catholic schools and Jewish schools for years.

But Islamic schools like the one in Batley appeared to violate the principles of a liberal education, and the very ideas to which the school owed its existence. And because of the community's religious beliefs, so important to its members, the future prospects for the girls were reduced. Was that the choice they had made? Did the Asian community really want this kind of separate education anyway? And if it did, how many wanted it? Or was it only a few earnest and repressed believers, all men, frightened of England and their daughters' sexuality?

The house Delius was born in, in Bradford, was now the Council of Mosques, which looked after the interests of the Bradford Muslims. There are 60,000 Muslims and thirty Muslim organisations in Bradford. Chowdhury Khan, the President of the Council, told me about the relations between men and women in Islam and the problem of girls' schools.

He said there were no women in the Council because 'we respect them too much'. I mentioned that I found this a little perplexing, but he ignored me, adding that this is also why women were not encouraged to have jobs or careers.

'Women's interests,' he said confidently, 'are being looked after.'

'And the girls?'

After the age of twelve, he said, women should not mix with men. That was why more single-sex schools were required in

Bradford. The local council had agreed that this was desirable and would provide more single-sex schools when resources were available. He added that, despite the Labour Manifesto, Neil Kinnock approved of this.

I said I doubted this.

Anyway, he continued, the local Labour Party was lobbying for more single-sex schools after having tried, in the 1960s, to provide mixed-sex schools. But – and this he emphasised – the Council of Mosques wanted single-sex schools, *not* Islamic ones or racially segregated schools. He banged on his desk: 'No, no, no! No apartheid!'

He wanted the state to understand that, while Muslim children would inevitably become Westernised – they were reconciled to that – they still wanted their children to learn about Islam at school, to learn sub-continental languages and be taught the history, politics and geography of India, Pakistan and Bangladesh. Surely, he added, the white British would be interested in this too. After all, the relations between England and the sub-continent had always been closer than those between Britain and France, say.

I found Chowdhury Khan to be a difficult and sometimes strange man. But his values, and the values of the Council he represented, are fairly straightforward. He believes in the pre-eminent value of the family and, for example, the importance of religion in establishing morality. He also believes in the innately inferior position of women. He dislikes liberalism in all its forms, and is an advocate of severe and vengeful retribution against law-breakers.

These are extremely conservative and traditional views. But they are also, isolated from the specifics of their sub-continental context, the values championed by the New Right, among others. There were a number of interesting ironies developing.

Sex and Secularity

Introduction to
Collected Screenplays One
(2002)

To me writing for film is no different to writing for any other form. It is the telling of stories, only on celluloid. However, you are writing for a director and then for actors. Economy is usually the point; one objective of film writing is to make it as quick and light as possible. You can't put in whatever you fancy in the hope that a leisured reader might follow you for a while, as you might in a novel. In that sense films are more like short stories. The restrictions of the form are almost poetic, though most poems are not read aloud in cineplexes. Film is a broad art, which is its virtue.

Nevertheless, it didn't occur to any of us involved in *My Son the Fanatic*, for instance, that it would be either lucrative or of much interest to the general public. The film was almost a legacy of the 1960s and '70s, when one of the purposes of the BBC was to make cussed and usually provincial dramas about contemporary issues like homelessness, class and the Labour Party.

I had been aware since the early 1980s, when I visited Pakistan for the first time, that extreme Islam, or 'fundamentalism' – Islam as a political ideology – was filling a space where Marxism and capitalism had failed to take hold. To me this kind of Islam resembled neo-fascism or even Nazism: an equality of oppression for the masses with a necessary enemy – in this case 'the West' – helping to keep everything in place. When I was researching *The Black Album* and *My Son the Fanatic*, a young fundamentalist I met did compare his 'movement' to the IRA, to Hitler and to the Bolsheviks. I guess he had in mind the idea that small groups of highly motivated people could make a powerful political impact.

This pre-Freudian puritanical ideology certainly provided meaning and authority for the helpless and dispossessed. As importantly, it worked too, for those in the West who identified with them; for those who felt guilty at having left their 'brothers' behind in the Third World. How many immigrant families are there who haven't done that? Most of my family, for instance, have long since fled to Canada, Germany, the US and Britain; but some members refused to go. There can't have been a single middle-class family in Pakistan who didn't always have a bank account in the First World, 'just in case'. Those left behind are usually the poor, uneducated, weak, old and furious.

Fundamentalist Islam is an ideology that began to flourish in a conspicuous age of plenty in the West, and in a time of media expansion. Everyone could see via satellite and video not only how wealthy the West was, but how sexualised it had become. (All 'sex and secularity over there, yaar,' as I heard it put.) This was particularly shocking for countries that were still feudal. If you were in any sense a Third Worlder, you could either envy Western ideals and aspire to them, or you could envy and reject them. Either way, you could only make a life in relation to them. The new Islam is as recent as postmodernism.

Until recently I had forgotten Saeed Jaffrey's fruity line in *My Beautiful Laundrette,* 'Our country has been sodomised by religion, it is beginning to interfere with the making of making of money.' Jaffrey's lordly laundrette owner was contrasted with the desiccated character played by Roshen Seth, for whom fraternity is represented by rational socialism rather than Islam, the sort of hopeful socialism he might have learned at the LSE in London in the 1940s. It is a socialism that would have no hope of finding a base in either 1980s Britain, or in Pakistan.

What Hussein, Omar and even his lover Johnny have in common is the desire to be rich. Not only that: what they also want, which is one of the West's other projects, is to flaunt and demonstrate to others their wealth and prosperity. They want to show off. This will, of course, induce violent envy in some of the poor and dispossessed, and may even encourage their desire to kill the rich.

One of my favourite uncles, a disillusioned Marxist, and a template for the character played by Shashi Kapoor in *Sammy and Rosie Get Laid,* had, by the mid-1980s, become a supporter of Reagan and Thatcher. Every morning we'd knock around

Karachi, going from office to office, where he had friends, to be given tea. No one ever seemed too busy to talk. My uncle claimed that economic freedom was Pakistan's only hope. If this surprised me, it was because I didn't grasp what intellectuals and liberals in the Third World were up against. There was a mass of people for whom alternative political ideologies either had no meaning or were tainted with colonialism, particularly when Islamic grassroots organisation was made so simple through the mosques. For my uncle the only possible contrast to revolutionary puritanism had to be acquisition; liberalism smuggled in via materialism. So if Islam represented a new puritanism, progress would be corruption, through the encouragement of desire. But it was probably too late for this already; American materialism, and the dependence and quasi-imperialism that accompanied it, was resented and despised.

In Karachi there were few books written, films made or theatre productions mounted. If it seemed dull to me, still I had never lived in a country where social collapse and murder were everyday possibilities. At least there was serious talk. My uncle's house, a version of which appears in *My Beautiful Laundrette*, was a good place to discuss politics and books, and read the papers and watch films. In the 1980s American businessmen used to come by. My uncle claimed they all said they were in 'tractors'. They worked for the CIA; they were tolerated if not patronised, not unlike the old-style British colonialists the Pakistani men still remembered. No one thought the 'tractor men' had any idea what was really going on, because they didn't understand the force of Islam.

But the Karachi middle class had some idea, and they were worried. They were obsessed with their 'status' or their position. Were they wealthy, powerful leaders of the country, or were they a complacent parasitic class – oddballs, Western but not, Pakistani but not – about to become irrelevant in the coming chaos of disintegration?

A few years later, in 1989, the fatwa against Rushdie was announced and, although I saw my family in London, I didn't return to Karachi. I was told by the Embassy that my safety 'could not be guaranteed'. Not long after, when I was writing *The Black Album*, a fundamentalist acquaintance told me that killing Rushdie had become irrelevant. The point was that this was 'the first time the community has worked together. It won't be the last. We know our strength now.'

I have often been asked how it's possible for someone like me to carry two quite different world-views within, of Islam and the West: not, of course, that I do. Once my uncle said to me with some suspicion, 'You're not a Christian, are you?' 'No,' I said. 'I'm an atheist.' 'So am I,' he replied. 'But I am still Muslim.' 'A Muslim atheist?' I said, 'it sounds odd.' He said, 'Not as odd as being nothing, an unbeliever.'

Like a lot of queries put to writers, this question about how to put different things together is a representative one. We all have built-in and contrasting attitudes, represented by the different sexes of our parents, each of whom would have a different background and psychic history. Parents always disagree about which ideals they believe their children should pursue. A child is a cocktail of its parent's desires. Being a child at all involves resolving, or synthesising, at least two different worlds, outlooks and positions.

If it becomes too difficult to hold disparate material within, if this feels too 'mad' or becomes a 'clash', one way of coping would be to reject one part entirely, perhaps by forgetting it. Another way is to be at war with it internally, trying to evacuate it, but never succeeding, an attempt Farid makes in *My Son the Fanatic*. All he does is constantly reinstate an electric tension between differences – differences that his father can bear and even enjoy, as he listens to Louis Armstrong and speaks Urdu. My father, who had similar tastes to the character played by Om Puri, never lived in Pakistan. But, like a lot of middle-class Indians, he was educated by both mullahs and nuns, and developed an aversion to both. He came to love Nat King Cole and Louis Armstrong, the music of black American former slaves. It is this kind of complexity that the fundamentalist has to reject.

Like the racist, the fundamentalist works only with fantasy. For instance, there are those who like to consider the West to be only materialistic and the East only religious. The fundamentalist's idea of the West, like the racist's idea of his victim, is immune to argument or contact with reality. (Every self-confessed fundamentalist I have met was anti-Semitic.) This fantasy of the Other is always sexual, too. The West is re-created as a godless orgiastic stew of immoral copulation. If the black person has been demonised by the white, in turn the white is now being demonised by the militant Muslim. These fighting couples can't leave one another alone.

These disassociations are eternal human strategies and they are banal. What a fiction writer can do is show the historical forms they take at different times: how they are lived out day by day by particular individuals. And if we cannot prevent individuals believing whatever they like about others – putting their fantasies into them – we can at least prevent these prejudices becoming institutionalised or an acceptable part of the culture.

A few days after the September 11 attack on the World Trade Center, a film director friend said to me, 'What do we do now? There's no point to us. It's all politics and survival. How do the artists go on?'

I didn't know what to say; it had to be thought about.

Islamic fundamentalism is a mixture of slogans and resentment; it works well as a system of authority that constrains desire, but it strangles this source of human life too. But of course in the Islamic states, as in the West, there are plenty of dissenters and quibblers, and those hungry for mental and political freedom. These essential debates can only take place within a culture; they are what a culture is, and they demonstrate how culture opposes the domination of either materialism or puritanism. If both racism and fundamentalism are diminishers of life – reducing others to abstractions – the effort of culture must be to keep others alive by describing and celebrating their intricacy, by seeing that this is not only of value but a necessity.

8 November 2001

The Arduous Conversation Will Continue

The Guardian
(19 July 2005)

We no longer know what it is to be religious, and haven't for a while. During the past two hundred years sensible people in the West have contested our religions until they lack significant content and force. These religions now ask little of anyone and, quite rightly, play little part in our politics.

The truly religious, following the logic of submission to political and moral ideals, and to the arbitrary will of God, are terrifying to us and almost incomprehensible. To us 'belief' is dangerous and we don't like to think we have much of it.

Confronted by this, it takes a while for our 'liberalism' to organise itself into opposition and for us to consider the price we might have to pay for it. We also have little idea of what it is to burn with a sense of injustice and oppression, and what it is to give our lives for a cause, to be so desperate or earnest. We think of these acts as mad, random and criminal, rather than as part of a recognisable exchange of violences.

The burning sense of injustice that many young people feel as they enter the adult world of double standards and dishonesty shock those of us who are more knowing and cynical. We find this commendable in young people but also embarrassing. Consumer society has already traded its moral ideals for other satisfactions, and one of the things we wish to export, masquerading as 'freedom and democracy', is that very consumerism, though we keep silent about its consequences: addiction, alienation, fragmentation.

We like to believe we are free to speak about everything, but we are reluctant to consider our own deaths, as well as the meaning of murder. Terrible acts of violence in our own neighbourhood – not unlike terrible acts of violence which are 'outsourced', usually taking place in the poorest parts of the Third World – disrupt the smooth idea of 'virtual' war that we have adopted to conquer the consideration of death.

'Virtual' wars are conflicts in which one can kill others without either witnessing their deaths or having to take moral responsibility for them. The Iraq war, we were told, would be quick and few people would die. It is as though we believed that by pressing a button and eliminating others far away we would not experience any guilt or suffering – on our side.

By bullying and cajoling the media, governments can conceal this part of any war, but only for a while. If we think of children being corrupted by video games – imitation violence making them immune to actual violence – this is something that has happened to our politicians. Modern Western politicians believe we can murder real others in faraway places without the same thing happening to us, and without any physical or moral suffering on our part.

This is a dangerous idea. The only way out is to condemn all violence or to recognise that violence is a useful and important moral option in the world. Despite our self-deception, we are quite aware of how necessary it is, at times, to kill others to achieve our own ends and to protect ourselves. If we take this position we cannot pretend it is morally easy and seek to evade the consequences.

We were dragged into this illegal and depressing war by many lies and much dissembling. A substantial proportion of us were opposed to it. During wars ordinary citizens feel they lack information and moral orientation while governments act decisively and with brutality.

Governments may be representative but they and the people are not the same. In our disillusionment, it is crucial that we remind ourselves of this. States behave in ways that would shame an individual. Governments persuade individuals to behave in ways that individuals know are morally wrong. Therefore governments do not speak for us; we have our own voices, however muffled they may seem. If communities are not to be corrupted by the government, the only patriotism possible is one that refuses the banality of taking either side, and continues the arduous conversation. That is why we have literature, the theatre, newspapers – a culture, in other words.

War debases our intelligence and derides what we have called 'civilisation' and 'culture' and 'freedom'. If it is true that we have entered a spiral of violence, repression and despair that will take years to unravel, our only hope is moral honesty about what we have brought about.

And not only us. If we need to ensure that what we call 'civilisation' retains its own critical position towards violence, religious groups have to purge themselves of their own intolerant and deeply authoritarian aspects.

The body-hatred and terror of sexuality that characterise most religions can lead people not only to cover their bodies in shame but to think of themselves as human bombs. This criticism on both sides is the only way to temper an inevitable legacy of bitterness, hatred and conflict.

The Carnival of Culture

28 July 2005

Recently a friend sent me an article which he thought I'd find interesting, as it was an attempt to sustain a non-violent version of Islam, one in which meddling and manipulative clerics had no authority. Without the requirement of intermediaries, no one could come between you and God. The clerics were seen here as political figures, rather than the best interpreters of Islam. If these fanatics and fundamentalists had twisted the word of God for their own political ends, why shouldn't the Koran be reclaimed and reinterpreted by the better intentioned? This, the writer stated, was the only way for Islam to go.

In the early 1990s, after my first visit to Pakistan, where I'd had a taste of what it was like to live in a (more or less) theocratic state; after the fatwa against Salman Rushdie and, finally, the death of my father, I began to visit various London mosques. Perhaps I was trying to find something of my father there, but I was also beginning to research what became *The Black Album*, a novel which concerned a group of students, young radical Muslims in West London, who burn *The Satanic Verses* and, later, attack a bookshop. A film I wrote for the BBC, *My Son the Fanatic*, about a young man who becomes a fundamentalist while his father falls in love with a prostitute, also emerged from this material.

I believed that questions of race, identity and culture were the major issues post-colonial Europe had to face, and that intergenerational conflict was where these conflicts were being played out. The British-born children of immigrants were not only more religious and politically radical than their parents – whose priority had been to establish themselves in the new country – but they despised their parent's moderation and desire to 'compromise' with Britain. To them this seemed weak.

My father was an Indian Muslim who didn't care for Islam; his childhood hadn't been much improved by a strict schooling, and teachers with sticks. Towards the end of his life he preferred

Buddhism to Islam, as there was less aggression and punishment in it. ('And altogether less religion,' as he put it.) He had also become disillusioned with the political version of Islam, which my father's school friend, Zulfi Bhutto – who the liberal classes thought would become a democratic and secular leader in the new Pakistan – was introducing to Pakistan.

The mosques I visited, in Whitechapel and Shepherd's Bush, were nothing like any church I'd attended. The scenes, to me, were extraordinary, and I was eager to capture them in my novel. There would be passionate orators haranguing a group of people sitting on the floor. One demagogue would replace another, of course, but the 'preaching' went on continuously, as listeners of all races came and went. I doubt whether you'd see anything like this now, but there would be diatribes against the West, Jews, and – their favourite subject – homosexuals. In my naivety I wondered whether, at the end of his speech, the speaker might take questions or engage in some sort of dialogue with his audience. But there was nothing like this. Most of the audience for this sort of thing were, I noticed, under thirty years old.

I had the good sense to see what good material this was, and took notes, until, one afternoon, I was recognised, and four strong men picked me up and carried me out onto the street, telling me never to return.

Sometimes I would be invited to the homes of these young 'fundamentalists'. One of them had a similar background to my own: his mother was English, his father a Muslim, and he'd been brought up in a quiet suburb. Now he was married to a woman from the Yemen who spoke no English. Bringing us tea, she came into the room backwards, and bent over too, out of respect for the men. The men would talk to me of 'going to train' in various places, but they seemed so weedy and polite I couldn't believe they'd want to kill anyone.

What did disturb me was this. These men believed they had access to the Truth, as stated in the Koran. There could be no doubt – or even much dispute about moral, social and political problems – because God had the answers. Therefore, for them, to argue with the Truth was like trying to disagree with the facts of geometry. For them the source of all virtue and vice was the pleasure and displeasure of Allah. To be a responsible human being was to submit to this. As the Muslim writer Shabbir Akhtar put it in his book *A Faith for All Seasons*, 'Allah is the subject of faith and loving obedience, not of rational inquiry or purely discursive thought. Unaided human reason is inferior in status to the gift of faith. Indeed, reason is useful only in so far as it finds a use in the larger service of faith.'

I found these sessions so intellectually stultifying and claustrophobic that at the end I'd rush into the nearest pub and drink rapidly, wanting to reassure myself I was still in England.

It is not only in the mosques but also in so-called 'faith schools' that such ideas are propagated. The Blair government, while attempting to rid us of radical clerics, has pledged to set up more of these schools, as though a 'moderate' closed system is completely different to an 'extreme' one. This might suit Blair and Bush. A benighted, ignorant enemy, riddled with superstition, incapable of independent thought, and terrified of criticism, is easily patronised.

Wittgenstein compared ideas to tools, which you can use for different ends. Some open the world up. The idea that you can do everything with one tool is ridiculous. Without adequate intellectual tools and the ability to think freely, too many Muslims are incapable of establishing a critical culture which goes beyond a stifling Islamic paradigm. As the Muslim academic Tariq Ramadan states, 'Muslims now need, more than ever, to be self-critical. That means educating young Muslims in more than religious formalism.'

If the idea of multi-culturalism makes some people vertiginous, mono-culturalism – of whatever sort – is much worse. Political and social systems have to define themselves in terms of what they exclude, and conservative Islam is leaving out a lot. In New York recently, a Turkish woman told me that Islam was denying its own erotic heritage, as shown in the *Arabian Nights*, *The Perfumed Garden*, and the tales of Hamza. Indeed, the Arabic scholar, Robert Irwin, states, of the *Arabian Nights*, 'In the modern Middle East, with certain exceptions, the *Nights* is not regarded by Arab intellectuals as literature at all.'

It is not only sexuality which is being excluded here, but the whole carnival of culture which comes from human desire. Our stories, dreams, poems, drawings, enable us to experience ourselves as strange to ourselves. It is also where we think of how we should live.

You can't ask people to give up their religion; that would be absurd. Religions may be illusions, and they may betray infantile wishes in their desire for certainty, but these are important and profound illusions. But they will modify as they come into contact with other ideas. This is what an effective multi-culturalism is: not a superficial exchange of festivals and food, but a robust and committed exchange of ideas – a conflict which is worth enduring, rather than a war.

When it comes to teaching the young, we have the human duty to inform them that there is more than one book in the world, and more than one voice, and that if they wish to have their voices heard by others, everyone else is entitled to the same thing. These children deserve better than an education which comes from liberal guilt.